Henry John T. Hildyard

Historical Record of the 71st Regiment Highland Light Infantry

from its formation in 1777, under the title of the 73rd, or McLeod's highlanders, up to the year 1876

Henry John T. Hildyard

Historical Record of the 71st Regiment Highland Light Infantry
from its formation in 1777, under the title of the 73rd, or McLeod's highlanders, up to the year 1876

ISBN/EAN: 9783337250706

Printed in Europe, USA, Canada, Australia, Japan

Cover: Foto ©Andreas Hilbeck / pixelio.de

More available books at **www.hansebooks.com**

HISTORICAL RECORD

OF THE

71st REGIMENT HIGHLAND LIGHT INFANTRY,

FROM ITS FORMATION IN 1777, UNDER THE
TITLE OF THE

73RD, OR McLEOD'S HIGHLANDERS,

UP TO THE YEAR 1876.

COMPILED BY

LIEUTENANT HENRY J. T. HILDYARD,
71st *H.L.I.*

London:
HARRISON AND SONS, 59, PALL MALL,
Booksellers to the Queen, and H.R.H. the Prince of Wales.
1876.

SUCCESSION OF COLONELS

IN THE

71st HIGHLAND LIGHT INFANTRY.

1777. John Lord McLeod.
1789. The Hon. Wm. Gordon.
1803. Sir John Francis Cradock, G.C.B.
1809. Francis Dundas.
1824. Sir Gordon Drummond, G.C.B.
1829. Sir Colin Halkett, K.C.B.
1838. Sir Samuel Ford Wittingham.
1841. Sir Thomas Reynell, Bart., K.C.B.
1848. Sir Thomas Arbuthnot, K.C.B.
1849. Sir James Macdonell, K.C.B. and K.C.H.
1857. Sir Thomas Napier, K.C.B.
1863. The Hon. Charles Grey.
1871. Robert Law, K.H.
1874. The Hon. Sir George Cadogan, K.C.B.

The Seventy-first Highland Light Infantry bears the following honorary records of its varied services on the regimental colour and appointments:—

"Hindoostan," for its distinguished services in India, between 1780 and 1797.

"Cape of Good Hope," for its part in the capture of that colony in 1806.

"Roleia,"
"Vimiera,"
"Corunna,"
"Fuentes d'onor,"
"Almaraz,"
"Vittoria,"
"Pyrenees,"
"Nive,"
"Orthes,"
"Peninsula,"
} For its several actions in which it was engaged in Spain and the South of France from 1808 to 1814.

"Waterloo," for its share in that battle in 1815.

"Sevastopol."

"Central India."

HISTORY

OF THE

71ST HIGHLAND LIGHT INFANTRY,

Formerly numbered the 73rd Regiment, and called McLeod's Highlanders.

TOWARDS the end of the year 1777 every effort was made by the British Ministry to encourage the country to raise troops voluntarily for the prosecution of the war then being waged between Great Britain and her American Colonies. Liverpool, Manchester, Edinburgh, Glasgow, each raised a regiment of a thousand men at its own expense, and several independent companies were formed in Wales. In this manner 15,000 men were raised and presented to the State, of which upwards of two-thirds were obtained from Scotland, and principally from the Highland clans.

At this time Lord McLeod, the eldest son of the Earl of Cromarty, whose title had been attainted and his estates forfeited for his participation in the Rebellion of 1745, returned to England from Sweden, having attained in its service the rank of Lieutenant-General. Being well received by His Majesty King George II, and finding his influence in the Highlands still considerable, although destitute of property, he offered his services to raise a regiment. The offer was accepted, and such was the respect entertained for his family and name, that in a short time 840 Highlanders were recruited and marched to Elgin.

1778. Here they were joined by 236 Lowlanders, raised by Captains the Honorable John Lindsay, David Baird, James Fowlis, and other officers, and by 34 English and Irish, who had been recruited in Glasgow. They amounted in all to 1,100 men, and were embodied at Elgin under the name of McLeod's Highlanders in April 1778, where they were inspected by General Skene, and approved by him as an excellent hardy body of men, fitted for any service. Immediately after the completion of this battalion, letters of service were granted for the creation of a second battalion, which was raised in like manner, with nearly the same expedition and in equal numbers. There is no record extant to show the different nationalities of which this battalion was formed, but it is probable that its composition was very similar to that of the first battalion when raised. Thus in the course of a few months Lord McLeod from being an exile without fortune or British military rank, found himself at the head of upwards of 2,200 of his countrymen, of whom nearly 1,800 were from that district and neighbourhood in which his family had once possessed so much influence.

Each battalion consisted of 50 sergeants, 50 corporals, 20 drummers and fifers, 2 pipers, and 1,000 privates, and was officered as under.

Colonel, John Lord McLeod.

FIRST BATTALION.
Lieut.-Colonel, Duncan McPherson.

Majors.

| John Elphinston | James Mackenzie. |

Captains.

George Mackenzie.	Hugh Lamont.
Alexander Gilchrist	Hon. James Lindsay.
John Shaw.	David Baird.
Charles Dalrymple.	

Captain Lieutenant and Captain, David Campbell. 1778.

Lieutenants.

A. Geddes Mackenzie.
Hon. John Lindsay.
Abraham Mackenzie, *Adjt.*
Alexander Mackenzie.
James Robertson.
John Hamilton.
John Hamilton.
Lewis Urquhart.
George Ogilvie.
Innes Munro.

Simon Mackenzie.
Philip Melvill.
John Mackenzie.
John Borthwick.
William Gunn.
William Charles Gorrie.
Hugh Sibbald.
David Rainnie.
Charles Munro.

Ensigns.

James Duncan.
Simon Mackenzie.
Alexander Mackenzie.
John Sinclair.

George Sutherland.
James Thrail.
Hugh Dalrymple.

Chaplain, Colin Mackenzie.
Adjutant, Abraham Mackenzie.
Quartermaster, John Lytrott.
Surgeon, Alexander M'Dougall.

SECOND BATTALION.

Lieut.-Colonel, The Hon. George Mackenzie.

Majors.

Hamilton Maxwell | Norman McLeod.

Captains.

Hon. Colin Lindsay.
John McIntosh.
James Fowlis.
Robert Sinclair.

Mackay Hugh Baillie.
Stair Park Dalrymple.
David Ross.
Adam Colt.

Lieutenants.

- Norman Maclean.
- John Irving.
- Rod. Mackenzie, *senior.*
- Charles Douglas.
- Angus McIntosh.
- John Fraser.
- Robert Arbuthnot.
- David M'Cullock.
- Rod. Mackenzie, *junior.*
- Phineas M'Intosh.
- John Mackenzie, *senior.*
- Alexander Mackenzie.
- Phipps Wharton.
- Laughlan M'Laughlan.
- Kenneth Mackenzie.
- Murdoch Mackenzie.
- George Fraser.
- John Mackenzie, *junior.*
- Martin Eccles Lindsay.
- John Dallas.
- David Ross.
- William Erskine.

Ensigns.

- John Fraser.
- John M'Dougal.
- Hugh Gray.
- ohn Mackenzie.
- John Forbes.
- Æneas Fraser.
- William Rose.
- Simon Fraser, *Adjt.*

Chaplain, Æneas Macleod.
Adjutant, Simon Fraser.
Quartermaster, Charles Clark.
Surgeon. Andrew Cairncross.

The uniform of the regiment was red, with the regular Highland equipments.

It is worthy of remark that when first raised, there were no less than 19 officers in the regiment named Mackenzie. It is probable that the proportion of non-commissioned officers and privates of that name was equally large, owing to the fact of the regiment having, as already stated, been principally raised on the estates of the Earl of Cromarty, the father of Lord McLeod. These estates are now in the possession of the present Duchess of Sutherland, who is Countess of Cromarty in her own right.

After being embodied at Elgin, the first battalion 1778. remained there some weeks, and then marched to Fort 1st bat. George, where it was formed into ten companies. It embarked on the 8th of May, 1,100 strong, under Lord McLeod, for Portsmouth, where it was to be transhipped and accompany the East India Fleet. The passage, however, having occupied fifteen days, the fleet sailed before the arrival of the transports, which were then ordered to proceed to Guernsey and Jersey. Here the battalion disembarked, and remained until relieved by the Seventy-eighth Regiment on the 27th November. Embarking on board the transports which brought the latter, it was conveyed to Portsmouth, where it disembarked on the 10th December and marched to Petersfield, where it was quartered until the close of the year. Orders having been received for its embarkation for the East Indies, a mutiny occurred in one of the companies, owing to a rumour gaining ground that the men had been sold to the East India Company by the British Government. This was happily checked, by the prompt and resolute spirit displayed by the officers, and the assurance of their Colonel that this report was entirely groundless. In January the battalion, about 1,100 strong, embarked on board Indiamen, under the command of Colonel Lord McLeod. Three vessels formed part of a fleet, escorted by Rear-Admiral Sir Edward Hughes, which in its passage touched at Goree, on the Coast of Africa, and captured that settlement from the French. After leaving Goree the fleet proceeded to the Cape of Good Hope, at that time in possession of the Dutch, where it landed its sick. It remained there three months, anchored in Table Bay, and then continued its course to India. The voyage, though tedious, was on the whole prosperous, and was brought to a close by anchor being dropped in Madras Roads on the 20th January, 1780, just twelve months subsequent to embarkation. The

1780.
1st bat. battalion was landed without delay at Fort St. George, where it remained about a month in barracks, after which it was removed to Poonamallee.

2nd bat. Before following the proceedings of the first battalion any further, it will be as well to return to the second battalion, which, as already mentioned, was embodied in September, 1778. In March of the following year, this battalion, 1,000 strong, and commanded by Lieut.-Colonel the Hon. George Mackenzie (brother of Lord McLeod), embarked at Fort George, and was conveyed to Plymouth. There it remained encamped upon Maker Heights until the 27th November, when it embarked for Gibraltar in transports under convoy of Admiral Sir George Brydges Rodney. In the Bay of Biscay the Spanish Caraccas Fleet was encountered, and captured, and the Admiral being compelled to employ a number of the men of his ships of war to man the prizes, called upon Lieut.-Colonel Mackenzie for the services of the battalion as Marines. A few days after the men had been distributed in this manner, the fleet fell in with the Spanish Admiral Don Juan de Langara, with a fleet consisting of eleven sail of the line, the whole of whose ships were either taken or dispersed. On the 18th January, 1780, the second battalion disembarked at Gibraltar, then closely blockaded by the Spaniards, landing at the New Mole and occupying the Casemates in the King's Bastion, the marching in strength being as follows :—

   30 Officers,   22 Drummers,
    6 Staff ditto,   944 Rank and file,
   50 Sergeants.

Here it remained during the whole of the siege of that fortress by the French and Spaniards, sustaining a high character as steady and trustworthy soldiers.

In the grand sortie in which the Spanish batteries before

the garrison were destroyed, all the grenadier and light
infantry companies in garrison were made up to their
establishment previous to the sortie. The grenadier and
light companies in this regiment consisted of four officers,
five sergeants, and 101 rank and file each. They were
stationed with the companies of the Thirty-ninth and
Fifty-sixth Regiments, and a proportion of artillery and
engineers, amounting in all to 668 men, in the centre, or
reserve column, commanded by Lieut.-Colonel Dachen-
hausen and Major Maxwell. The orders they received
were to march through Bayside barrier, towards the mortar
batteries. The moon shone brightly as the soldiers
assembled on the sands at midnight. Between two and
three o'clock darkness overspread the country, and the
troops issued silently from the fortress. They were chal-
lenged and fired upon by the enemy's sentries, but the
British soldiers rushed forward, overpowered the Spanish
guards, and captured the batteries. The enemy's soldiers,
instead of defending the works, fled in dismay and communicated the panic to the troops in their rear. Within an
hour the object of the sortie was effected. trains were laid
to the enemy's magazines, and the soldiers withdrew. As
they entered the fortress, tremendous explosions shook the
ground, and rising columns of smoke, flame, and burning
timber proclaimed the destruction of the enemy's immense
stores of gunpowder. General Elliot stated in orders :—

1780.
2nd bat.

" The bearing and conduct of the whole detachment,
" officers, seamen and soldiers on this glorious occasion,
" surpass my utmost acknowledgements." The casualties
in the three columns of attack were only 4 killed, 24
wounded, and 1 missing. The grenadier company, commanded by Captain Sinclair on this occasion, drove the
enemy from their centre guard-house, and the light infantry,
commanded by Captain Dalrymple, obliged them to
evacuate Parchal's battery.

30.   The casualties of the battalion during the three years
bat. that the siege lasted were 1 sergeant, 41 privates killed; 6 officers, 7 sergeants, and 108 rank and file wounded, and 58 privates died from sickness. Although application has frequently been made to the authorities, for permission to have Gibraltar inscribed on the colours, yet for some inexplicable reason, this has always been refused, though granted to other regiments that served during the siege with the Seventy-third.

In May, 1783, it embarked on board transports, and sailed for Portsmouth, where it landed in July, and occupied Hilsea Barracks. The following month it marched to Stirling, where it was disbanded on the 3rd October after a service of five years, during the whole of which period it was commanded by Lieut.-Colonel the Hon. George Mackenzie.

In 1784 the officers belonging to the late second battalion who were regimentally senior to those serving with the first were given the option of joining that battation in the East Indies at their own expense, of which some availed themselves.

bat.   We shall now return to the first battalion which we left in quarters at Poonamallee in February, 1780. At the commencement of 1780 a new war had broken out in India, the causes of which it is not easy to unravel, owing to the depth to which the several Presidencies of the East India Company had entered into the intrigues and quarrels of the Native rulers. On the 5th April, the Mahratta Chiefs, Holkar and Scindia, were defeated in their camp whilst advancing on Surat, and this victory was followed by numerous less important successes. In Bengal, military movements were taking place under the direction of Sir Eyre Coote, who had now succeeded to the chief command in India, and the strong fortress of Gwalior, hitherto regarded as impregnable, was taken by escalade on the 3rd August.

On the side of Madras the forces on the establishment 1780. did not exceed 30,000 men, dispersed in very distant quarters, and the Presidency had unfortunately been engrossed in internal disputes rather than in active measures of preparation to oppose the enemy. Such was the state of affairs at Madras when on the 10th of June information was received that a large army was assembling at Bangalore under Hyder Ali, the son of a petty chief in Mysore, who had risen to the chief command of the army of that State. On the death of the Rajah, Hyder Ali assumed the guardianship of his eldest son, who was left a minor, placing him under restraint, and seizing upon the reins of government. Having a considerable territory under his control, he maintained a formidable military establishment, which he endeavoured to bring into a high state of discipline and efficiency. Standing now in the position of Sultan of Mysore, he formed a league with the French, and entered into a confederacy with the Nizam of the Deccan, the Mahrattas, and other native powers, for the purpose of expelling the British from India.

In July, 1780, Hyder Ali, having passed the Ghauts, burst like a torrent into the Carnatic, whilst his son, Tippoo Saïb, advanced with a large body of cavalry against the Northern Circars, and even the villages near Madras were attacked by parties of the enemy's horse. In consequence of these events the first battalion Seventy-third Regiment was ordered to join the army being assembled at St. Thomas's Mount under the command of Major-General Sir Hector Munro, K.B. This army amounted to upwards of 4,000 men, consisting entirely of the Honourable East India Company's troops, with the exception of the Seventy-third Highlanders, then about 800 strong. It was composed as follows:—

European	Infantry	1,000
	Artillery	300
	Dragoons	30
Native	Infantry	3,250
	Dragoons	30
	Total	4,610

Attached to these were 30 field pieces and howitzers, and four battering 24-pounders.

On the 25th August this corps marched to Conjeveram, about 50 miles west of Madras on the Arcot road, where it was to be met by a body of men under Colonel Baillie, from the Gunton Circar, the joint force proceeding to raise the siege of Arcot, invested by Hyder Ali on the 21st August. Sir Hector Munro's army arrived at Conjeveram on the 29th August, being followed the whole way by the enemy's horse. The country here was found to be entirely under water, so that no provisions of any kind were to be procured, and the force was consequently dependent upon the four day's provisions in its possession.

Hyder Ali now raised the siege of Arcot, and detached Tippoo Saib with a force of 40,000 horse and foot and 12 guns to intercept Colonel Baillie and prevent his junction with the main army. This junction had been expected to take place on the 30th August, but Baillie being delayed some days by the sudden rising of a small river, this time was utilised by the enemy to intercept him.

Colonel Baillie reached Perambaucum, 15 miles from General Munro's position, on the 6th September, where he was attacked by Tippoo Saïb, whom after a contest of several hours he repulsed. Strange to say, however, the forces of Munro and Baillie, though within a few hours' march of each other, made no effort to unite. Two days after the battle, Colonel Baillie sent notice to General

Munro to push forward with the main body, as, from the loss he had lately sustained and from want of provisions, he was unable to advance in the face of an enemy so superior in numbers. After this unaccountable delay, the General sent forward a detachment under Colonel Fletcher consisting of the flank companies Seventy-third (now Seventy-first), two companies of European grenadiers, and 11 companies of Sepoys, in all 1,000 men. Of the flank companies, Seventy-third, the grenadier company was commanded by Lieutenant the Hon. John Lindsay, and the light company by Captain, afterwards General the Right Hon. Sir David Baird, G.C.B. Colonel Fletcher joined Colonel Baillie's force on the 9th September.

Reinforced by this detachment, Colonel Baillie set out to join Munro on the same evening, but had not proceeded beyond a mile when he fell in with the pickets of Hyder Ali's army. An irregular fire commenced, which was kept up by both parties for several miles, until Colonel Baillie halted about midnight, when he lay on his arms all night without being disturbed by the enemy.

He continued his march next morning without opposition, and after proceeding two miles entered a jungle. The Sultan had concentrated his army about this spot, and on the preceding day had thrown up three batteries, one in the centre of the grove and one on each flank. No sooner had Colonel Baillie entered the jungle than a heavy and destructive fire was opened upon him from 57 pieces of cannon. The march was continued in the form of a square, with the sick, baggage, and ammunition in the centre; and though the detachment was assailed on all sides by an immense force, the enemy after a desperate conflict of three hours' duration, was driven back at every point.

Thus repulsed, Hyder Ali determined to retreat, and orders had been given to Colonel Lally, a French officer

1780. in the service of the Sultan, to draw off his men, and to the cavalry to cover the retreat, when two explosions were seen to take place in the British line. These laid open one entire face of their column, destroyed their artillery, and threw the whole into irreparable confusion. This occurrence revived Hyder's hopes, his cavalry charged in successive squadrons, and his infantry poured volleys of musketry upon the devoted band. Reduced at length to little more than 400 men, Colonel Baillie formed these into a square upon a small eminence. Here, after two-thirds of the number had been killed or disabled, the officers with their swords, and the soldiers with their bayonets, repulsed thirteen charges. At length, borne down by fresh bodies of horse, Colonel Baillie, to save the lives of the few brave men who survived, displayed a flag of truce. Quarter was promised, but no sooner had the men laid down their arms, than they were savagely attacked, and only by the humane interference of the French officers were any lives saved.

One of these officers,* speaking of this action says :—
" Too great encomiums cannot be bestowed on the English
" commander and his troops, for in the whole of this trying
" conflict they preserved a coolness of manœuvre which
" would have done honour to any troops in the world.
" Raked by the fire of an immense artillery, the greater
" part of the action within grape shot range, attacked on
" all sides by not less than 25,000 horse and 30 battalions
" of Sepoys, besides Hyder's European troops, the English
" column stood firm, and repulsed every charge with great
" slaughter. The horse driven back on the foot, the right
" of our line began to give way, though composed of the
" best troops in the Mysore army."

In this action, known by the name of the battle of

---

* Journal of a French officer.

Perambaucum, Lieut.-Colonel Fletcher and 29 European **1780.** officers, with 155 rank and file were killed; Lieut.-Colonel Baillie with 34 officers, and almost all the European privates, were wounded; 16 officers and privates remained unhurt, who, with the rest, were made prisoners. The whole of the sepoys were either killed, taken, or dispersed.

From the report of an eye-witness, it is stated that the grenadiers of this regiment under Captain Baird fought with such determination and heroism, that many of them were seen loading their muskets after their legs had been shot away; almost all disdained to accept of quarter.

The flank companies were almost annihilated. Lieut. Geddes Mackenzie and William Gunn, Volunteer Forbes, 3 sergeants, and 82 rank and file were killed. Captain Baird received seven wounds, and Lieutenant the Hon. John Lindsay nine. Lieutenants Philip Melville and Hugh Cuthbert, 4 sergeants, 4 drummers, and 92 rank and file were also wounded. All these, with 23 who escaped without wounds, were thrown into a dungeon by Hyder Ali, where they were treated with such barbarity that only 30 of the soldiers survived, and of these few were afterwards fit for service.

Mrs. Grant, in her "Superstitions of the Highlanders," referring to this in allusion to the inflexible integrity of the Highlanders under the most trying circumstances, says of the prisoners:—

"They were treated with the most cruel indignity, and "fed upon sparing proportions of unwholesome rice, which "operated as a slow poison, assisted by the burning heat "of the sun by day, and the unwholesome dews of night, "to which they were purposely exposed to shake their "constancy. Daily some of their companions dropped "before their eyes, and daily they were offered liberty and "riches in exchange for this lingering torture, on condition

1780. " of relinquishing their religion and taking the turban.
" These Highlanders were entirely illiterate, scarce one of
" them could have told the name of any particular sect of
" Christians, and all the idea they had of the Mahommedan
" religion was that it was adverse to their own, and to
" what they had been taught by their fathers."

Of the two entire companies but two men rejoined the battalion, and these were found in the jungle desperately wounded. In consequence of this, two new flank companies were formed from the battalion by Lord McLeod.

After Colonel Baillie's defeat, Sir Hector Munro retired with the army to Chingleput, being much pressed by the enemy during his march. The sick and wounded being left there, the army went into quarters on Choultry Plain for the rainy season, which had now set in.

During the retreat the troops suffered severely from fatigue and want of provisions. Captain Gilchrist, of the grenadiers, whose ill health had prevented his being with his company, died, and Lieutenant Alexander Mackenzie, with a great many privates, was wounded in skirmishes with the enemy.

1781. Upon the 17th January the army, being reassembled, took the field under the command of Lieutenant-General Sir Eyre Coote. At this time the strength of the regiment did not exceed 500 men, and was commanded by Lieutenant-Colonel James Craufurd, this officer having succeeded Lord McLeod, who relinquished his command, and returned to England, having, it is said, differed in opinion with General Munro on the subject of his movements. Hyder Ali was in the Tanjore country committing every species of outrage and devastation.

On the 1st June, 1781, Colonel Lord McLeod received the local rank of Major-General in the East Indies. In June Sir Eyre Coote moved his force southwards along the coast towards Cuddalore, where his outposts were attacked by Tippoo Saïb, who was repulsed. He afterwards moved to Chillumborem, upon the Coleroon, where the enemy had a large magazine of grain. The Pagoda was attacked by the pickets under Major John Shaw, Seventy-third Highlanders, but they were repulsed and that officer wounded.

1781.

Hyder Ali, apprehensive for the safety of Chillumborem, moved his army in that direction from Tanjore and Trichinopoly, whilst Lieutenant-General Sir Eyre Coote, with the view of obtaining supplies from the shipping, proceeded towards Cuddalore. By forced marches and manœuvres, however, Hyder Ali succeeded in nearly surrounding the latter on the plains of Porto Novo, about two days' march south of Cuddalore.

About 4 a.m. on the 1st of July, the enemy, whose force was computed at 25 battalions of infantry, 400 Europeans, 45,000 horse, and above 100,000 matchlock-men, peons, and polygars, with 47 pieces of cannon, was seen to draw up in line of battle. The British force did not exceed 8,000 men, of which the Seventy-third was the only European regiment. Notwithstanding this immense disparity of force, Sir Eyre Coote determined to attack the enemy, and drew up his army in two lines, the first, of which the Seventy-third Highlanders formed a part, being commanded by Major-General Sir Hector Munro; the second by Major-General James Stuart. A plain divided the two armies, beyond which the enemy was drawn up on ground strengthened by front and flanking redoubts and batteries. The action commenced by an advanced movement of the English troops, and after eight hours' hard fighting the enemy was forced from all his intrenchments and compelled to retire. The Seventy-third was on the right of the first line, and led all the attacks to the full approbation of the general commanding. His attention was particularly attracted by one of the pipers, who always blew up more

1781. heartily the heavier the fire became. This so pleased the general that he cried out "Well done my brave fellow, you shall have a pair of silver pipes for this!" The promise was not forgotten, for a handsome pair of pipes was presented to the regiment, with an appropriate inscription bearing testimony to the general's esteem for its conduct and character. Meer Saïb, Hyder Ali's favourite general, was mortally wounded in this action, and amongst the 4,000 killed were many of his principal officers.

The results of this battle enabled Sir Eyre Coote to reach Cuddalore, his point of destination, on the 4th July, and soon afterwards the army was moved to St. Thomas's Mount. On the 3rd August the force from Bengal under the orders of Colonel Pearse, arrived and formed a junction with Sir Eyre Coote's army at Pulicat, to which place the army had moved to facilitate that object. The British force now amounted to 12,000 men; the 1st Brigade, composed entirely of Europeans, was commanded by Colonel Craufurd, Seventy-third Highlanders, and had its station generally in the centre of the line. Major-General Sir Hector Munro commanded the right wing, and Colonel Pearse the left. About this period died Major James Mackenzie, universally regretted by the regiment. His exertions in the early part of the campaign had brought on an illness, which terminated his valuable life.

On the 16th August the preparations which had been actively carried on for the siege of Arcot and the relief of Vellore being completed, the army was put in motion. On the 20th Tripassoor was retaken, and a large supply of grain found there. Hyder Ali's camp was now at Conjeveram, and every exertion was made by his detachments to check the progress of the troops. On the 27th August, the enemy was found drawn up in order of battle upon the very ground which had witnessed Colonel Baillie's defeat, a position which Hyder Ali's religious notions induced him to consider fortunate. Here he had determined to try the 1781. issue of a second general action, the result of which will be best told by the following extract from General Meadows' despatch :—

"Hyder thought proper to fall back a few miles to the
"ground on which he had defeated the detachment under
"Colonel Baillie, where he took up a strong position, and,
"influenced by a superstitious notion of its being a lucky
"spot, had determined, as I was informed by my intelli-
"gence, to try his fortune in a second battle. I accordingly
"marched on the 27th, in the morning, towards him, and,
"as reported, about 8 o'clock we discovered his army in
"order of battle and in full force to receive us, and in
"possession of many strong and advantageous posts, ren-
"dered the more formidable by the nature of the country
"lying between, which was intersected by very deep
"watercourses; in short, nothing could be more formidable
"than the situation of the enemy, and nothing more
"arduous than our approach to present a front to them.
"I was obliged to form the line under a heavy cannonade
"from several batteries, as well as from the enemy's line,
"which galled us exceedingly, and was a very trying situa-
"tion for the troops, who bore it with firmness and un-
"daunted bravery, which did draw the highest honour and
"showed a steady valour not to be surpassed by the first
"veterans of any nation in Europe. The conflict lasted
"from nine in the morning till near sunset, when we had
"driven the enemy from all their strong posts, and obliged
"them to retreat with precipitation, leaving us in full pos-
"session of the field of battle." The loss of the British was upwards of 400 killed and wounded, almost all being native troops.

There was one circumstance peculiar to this field of battle, which stamped it with aggravated horrors. It is described by Captain Munro in his narrative as follows :—

1781. " Perhaps there come not within the wide range of human
" imagination scenes more affecting or circumstances more
" touching than many of our army had that day to witness
" and to bear. On the very spot where they stood lay
" strewed amongst their feet the relics of their dearest
" fellow-soldiers and friends, who near twelve months before
" had been slain by the hands of those very inhuman
" monsters that now appeared a second time eager to com-
" plete the work of blood. One poor soldier, with the tear
" of affection glistening in his eye, picked up the decaying
" spatterdash of his valued brother, with the name yet
" entire upon it, which the tinge of blood and effects of
" weather had kindly spared. . . . . The scattered
" clothes and wings of the flank companies were everywhere
" perceptible, as also their helmets and skulls, both of
" which bore the marks of many furrowed cuts."

Upon this spot the army halted two days, and it then retired to Tripassoor, to secure provisions. At this period the health of Major General Sir Hector Munro compelled him to leave the army, which led to Colonel Craufurd becoming second in command, the charge of the regiment devolving upon Major John Shaw.

On the 27th September, near Sholingar, Colonel Craufurd received the Commander-in-Chief's orders to move the British Army to the front. Hyder Ali, confident of success, made a forward movement to meet it, when a general action ensued. A detachment commanded by Colonel Edmonstone, and of which the flank companies Seventy-third formed a part, succeeded in turning the enemy's left flank, and falling upon his camp and rear. The day closed with the total defeat of Hyder Ali's troops, who were pursued by the cavalry until sunset.

On the 1st October, under circumstances the most distressing and unpromising, but with a hope of obtaining provisions, of which the army was quite destitute, and for

which no previous arrangement had been made by the 1781.
Government, Sir Eyre Coote pushed boldly through the
Sholingar Pass, and after a march of two days encamped
at Altamancherry, in the Polygar country. Here, by the
friendly aid and kindness of Bum Raze, one of the Polygar
princes, the troops were well supplied with every requisite.
The British camp was moved to Pollipat on the 26th
October, and the sick and wounded sent to Tripassoor.
Vellore was also relieved, after which the army, reinforced
by Colonel Laing with 100 Europeans from Vellore, proceeded to the attack of Chittoor, which, after a gallant
resistance, capitulated. With a view to draw his opponents
from so·inaccessible a country, Hyder Ali proceeded to
the attack of Tripassoor, and on the 20th November Sir
Eyre Coote retired out of the Pollamo, through the
Naggary Pass, which obliged the enemy to raise the siege
of Tripassoor and retire on Arcot. The campaign closed
with the recapture of Chittoor by the enemy. On the
2nd December, the monsoon having set in, the army broke
up its camp on the Koilatoor Plain, and the different
corps marched into cantonments in the neighbourhood of
Madras.

At the opening of the succeeding campaign at the 1782.
beginning of 1782, the army did not muster a larger force
than at the commencement of the former year. The first
and most important object in view was the relief of Vellore,
kept in strict blockade by the enemy. The safety of this
fortress was of paramount consequence, being the only
key possessed by the British to the passes of the Ghauts,
through which an invasion of the enemy's country could
alone be accomplished. The army pushed through the
Sholingar Pass, and by the 11th January Vellore was
relieved and supplied with rice for six months. After this
was effected the army retired, and on the 20th January
arrived at Poonamallee, having lost upon this expedition

1782. 6 officers and about 30 Europeans, with 100 Sepoys killed and wounded.

The following account of the death of John Mackay, a corporal of the battalion, in a skirmish with the enemy on the march to Vellore, is given by Captain Munro:—" For " the satisfaction of my Highland friends, I take this oppor- " tunity of commemorating the fall of John Mackay, alias " Donn, a corporal in the Seventy-third, son of Robert Donn, " the famous Highland bard, whose singular talent for the " beautiful and extemporaneous composition of Gaelic " poetry was held in such esteem by the Highland Society. " This son of the bard has frequently revived the drooping " spirits of his countrymen upon the march by singing in a " pleasant manner the humorous and lively productions of " his father. He was killed by a cannon ball on the 13th " of January, and on the same evening was interred by his " disconsolate comrades with all the honours of war."

For the first three months of the year 1782 the army of Lieutenant-General Sir Eyre Coote was retained inactive at St. Thomas' Mount, the government of the presidency being apprehensive for its own safety, whereas a judicious movement on Porto Novo might have prevented Tippoo Saïb's junction with the strong reinforcement of French troops that had arrived from Europe in Admiral Suffrein's fleet, or at least averted the loss of Permacoil and Cuddalore. At length Sir Eyre Coote, having been reinforced by the Seventy-eighth (afterwards the Seventy-second) Regiment from England, was allowed to commence operations.

At the beginning of April he marched in a southerly direction by Corangooly and Wandewash towards the enemy, encamped upon the Red Hills of Pondicherry. The object of the Commander-in-Chief appeared to be to separate the French from the Mysore troops, for which purpose he manœuvred between Chitaput and Arnee, where he had established magazines. Hyder Ali made a rapid movement, on the 2nd of June overtaking and attack- 1782. ing the British rear guard, commanded by Lieutenant-Colonel John Elphinston,* Seventy-third Highlanders, who maintained his ground with great spirit and intrepidity until the line had completed its formation. The troops were then ordered to advance immediately upon the enemy's guns, and the foe was soon forced across the River Arnee, and in pursuit several tumbrils were taken by Captain the Honourable James Lindsay. This officer, perceiving a battalion of the enemy extricating the tumbrils from the bed of the river, dashed forward at the head of his grenadier company, supported by the remainder of the corps under Major-General Mackenzie, and succeeded in dispersing the enemy and seizing the tumbrils. The conduct of Captain Lindsay, although he had acted without orders, received the commendation of the Commander-in-Chief. At the action of Arnee the staff of the regimental colour was shattered by a cannon ball, and the ensign carrying it was severely wounded.

The army encamped for the night on the field of battle, and on the following morning took up a position before Arnee; but a scarcity of grain compelled the General to retrace his steps towards Madras, and on the 20th of June he arrived at St. Thomas's Mount.

In the months of July and August the army made two expeditions, one to Wandewash, in which it was foiled by the activity of Hyder Ali, the other for the relief of Vellore, which was more fortunate, as it succeeded in throwing a large quantity of grain into the fortress. The siege of Cuddalore being determined on, the army moved on the 26th August in a southerly direction, and on the 4th September halted on the Red Hills of Pondicherry. Deserters reported the garrison of Cuddalore to consist of 800 Euro-

---

* Major in the Seventy-third, Lieut.-Colonel by "local" rank, dated 23rd May, 1781.

1782. peans, 300 Africans, and 600 Sepoys, who having expelled the inhabitants, and covered the walls with cannon were resolved to defend the place to the last extremity. The failure of the supplies which Sir Eyre Coote had been led to expect from Madras by the fleet, excited so much anxiety and disappointment in the veteran's mind, that a severe illness ensued, which obliged him to quit the army. The command devolved upon Major-General James Stuart, who commenced his retreat on the evening of the 10th October. On the 15th October, the monsoon set in with unusual severity, and the army went into cantonments in the vicinity of Madras. Hyder Ali at the same time resumed his old position near Arcot. Shortly after this, Rear-Admiral Sir Richard Bickerton, with a large fleet from England, arrived in Madras Roads. Considerable reinforcements were on board, consisting of the Twenty-third Light Dragoons, One hundred and first and One hundred and second Regiments, and the Fifteenth Regiment of Hanoverian Infantry, which joined the army in its cantonments.

In December occurred the death of Hyder Ali, who was, however, succeeded without commotion by his son Tippoo Saïb, to whom he left a kingdom of his own acquisition, which made him one of the most powerful princes in India. Notwithstanding that by private information overland news was received of a peace having been concluded between England and the other belligerent powers in Europe, still the Madras Government determined to persevere in its original plans for the attack of Cuddalore. With this view Major-General Stuart put his army in
1783. motion on the 21st April, marching by brigades in a southerly direction. It consisted of the Seventy-third and Seventy-eighth, and One hundred and first regiments, a considerable body of native troops, and a detachment of Hanoverians under Colonel Wangenheim. Brevet Lieu-

tenant-Colonel Elphinston, Seventy-third Highlanders, took the lead with the Fifth brigade, to the command of which he had been appointed, in consideration of his distinguished conduct and important services in the field. Lieut.-Colonel James Stuart, Seventy-eighth Highlanders, commanded the First or European Brigade, of which the Seventy-third formed a part, and which amounted to 1,600 men. Colonel Elphinston in his advance possessed himself of the Permacoil ruins, from whence the enemy's advanced parties could be plainly seen upon the Red Hills. The remainder of the army joined him there on the 2nd May. About this time accounts were received of the death of Lieut.-General Sir Eyre Coote, and Major-General Stuart temporarily succeeded to the command of the forces in India.

After leaving Permacoil, the army advanced to Killinoor, and from thence towards the Red Hills. On the 4th June, Major-General Stuart encamped close to the Pannar river, about five miles west of Cuddalore, behind which the French army was descried in an intrenched camp. The British passed the Pannar river on the 6th June without opposition, passed the Bandipollam Hills, and took up a strong position not more than two miles from the south face of the fortress of Cuddalore, having the right flank covered by the sea and the left by the Bandipollam Hills. The enemy, commanded by General de Bussy, had in the meantime thrown up works along his front. On the 12th June Major-General Stuart determined to attack General de Bussy in the position he occupied, and issued preparatory orders accordingly. At 4 o'clock on the morning of the 13th June the action commenced by a movement from the British left against the enemy's right flank. A very obstinate and sanguinary contest ensued, continuing without intermission until the evening, when, both armies remaining upon the field of battle, each claimed the victory.

1783.

1783. In this action the Seventy-third Highlanders highly distinguished itself, having wrested from the enemy in the course of the conflict seven different redoubts. The loss it sustained was very severe, amounting in killed and wounded to 13 officers and 272 men, being one-half of the number in the field. The regiment was commanded by Captain Hugh Lamont. Captain the Honourable James Lindsay, commanding the Grenadier Company, Captain Alexander McKenzie, Lieuts. Simon Mackenzie and James Trail, 4 sergeants and 80 rank and file were killed. Captain John Hamilton, Lieuts. Charles Gorrie, David Rannie, John Sinclair, James Duncan, and George Sutherland, 5 sergeants and 107 rank and file were wounded. The enemy's loss was estimated at 62 officers, 961 men killed, wounded, and missing.

The following flattering compliment formed part of the General Orders issued by the Commander-in-Chief at the conclusion of the action:—

"I am also grateful to Captain Lamont and the officers
" under his command who gallantly led the *precious remains*
" of the Seventy-third Highlanders through the most
" perilous road to glory, until exactly one-half of the
" officers and men were either killed or wounded."

The British prosecuted the siege of Cuddalore with vigour, and on the 25th June the first parallel was completed. On that day the enemy made a sortie, but was repulsed with considerable loss after a severe contest. The commander of the party, Colonel le Chevalier de Damas, was among the prisoners taken. On the 1st July a frigate arrived in Cuddalore Roads, bringing official accounts from England of a general peace having been concluded, and hostilities consequently ceased.

By the 2nd August the British army had received the supplies, of which it stood greatly in want, and the camp was broken up, the troops marching to St. Thomas's Mount where they arrived on the 16th August. Shortly afterwards, the army went into winter quarters, the Seventy-third occupying the fort and cantonment of Arcot. On the conclusion of the peace, in March, 1784, Captains Baird and the Honble. John Lindsay, Lieut. Melville and about 30 men, who were taken in Colonel Baillie's affair, were released and rejoined the regiment. During the remainder of the year the Seventy-third continued at Arcot, and was only employed, beyond the usual routine of duty in quarters, for a short time in quelling a mutiny which broke out in the native cavalry at Arnee. The regiment at this period was commanded by Lieut.-Colonel William Dalrymple. In the course of the month of June it was removed from Arcot to Fort St. George, where it was joined by several officers of the late second battalion, which had been disbanded. Lieut.-Colonel Dalrymple having returned to England, Lieut.-Colonel the Honble. George Mackenzie took command of the regiment, which continued in quarters at Madras for the remainder of the year.*

1784.

At the commencement of the year 1786, the numerical title of the regiment was changed to the Seventy-first Highlanders, and new colours were received from England bearing that number, which designation it has since retained. In March quarters were changed to Wallajahabad and Chingleput, nine companies being cantoned at the former and one at the latter under Brevet Lieut.-Colonel Hamilton Maxwell.

On the 4th June, 1787, Colonel the Honble. George Mackenzie, commanding the regiment, died after a short illness and was interred at Madras. He was succeeded in the command by the senior major, Brevet Lieut.-Colonel

---

* The effective return of the regiment at this time was 29 officers, 934 sergeants, rank and file.

John Elphinston, who was succeeded in the majority by Captain David Baird.

During the year 1787 no change of quarters took place.

1788. In February, 1788, in consequence of some disturbance or alarm in the Bombay presidency, the Seventy-first, about 800 strong, marched to Madras, and immediately embarked on board the Company's ships for Bombay, where it arrived in April after a favourable passage. It remained here only six months, when, its services being dispensed with, it returned to Madras, and arrived there in December. Five companies under Lieut.-Colonel Elphinston occupied the barracks in Fort St. George, and the other five companies proceeded to Poonamallee. Major-General the Honble. William Gordon was appointed Colonel on the 9th April, 1789, in succession to Major-General John Lord McLeod deceased. In the course of the year the five companies at Poonamallee were moved to Tripassoor.

1790. Early in 1790, hostilities having commenced by Tippoo Sultan attacking and capturing the lines of Travancore, the British Government in India determined to support the Rajah of that country. On the 18th of March an encampment was formed for that purpose in the neighbourhood of Conjeveram under the command of Colonel Musgrave. The force assembled there consisted of the Nineteenth British Dragoons, the Fifty-second and Seventy-first Highlanders, the Third and Fourth Regiments of native Cavalry, the first Battalion of Coast Artillery, and five of Coast Infantry. On the 29th of March this force moved to Trichinopoly, where Colonel Musgrave effected a junction on the 29th April, with the division assembled there under Colonel Brydges. This comprised the Thirty-sixth and Seventy-second Regiments, the Second and Fifth Native Cavalry, and seven battalions of Coast Sepoys.

On the 24th of May General Meadows arrived at Trichinopoly, and assumed the command : the army consisted of 15,000 men, forming two European and four native brigades. These were divided into wings. Lieut.-Colonel James Stuart, Seventy-second Highlanders, being appointed to command the left wing, and Colonel Brydges of the East India Company's Service, the right; the Seventy-first and Seventy-second Highlanders, and First East India Company's European battalion, formed the Second European brigade, under Lieut.-Colonel Clarke of the Company's Service. The whole of the cavalry in the advance was commanded by Lieut.-Colonel Sir John Floyd of the Nineteenth Light Dragoons.

1790.

On the 24th May, Major-General (afterwards Sir William) Meadows reviewed the army, which on the 26th was moved towards the Coimbatore country by Anatore and Kidnaveran, On the 15th June the army reached the fortified post of Caroor, which the enemy abandoned without opposition. Here it remained strengthening the place and collecting grain till the 2nd July, when it moved to Arrivacourchy, where it arrived on the 5th, and, continuing its march by Toorambuddy, reached Daraporam on the 10th July, where a large supply of grain was found. The army arrived at Coimbatore on the 22nd July, being harassed on the march by Tippoo Saïb's irregular horse. A halt was made here, and detachments sent to reduce Dindigul, Errode, and Palghautcherry, upon which service the flank companies of the Seventy-first were employed under Captains Phineas McIntosh and James Robertson. In August the whole of the cavalry and the advanced infantry had been pushed forward to the Boovany, near to the Gudzelhetty Pass. Tippoo Saïb, profiting by the divided state of the British force, descended with his whole army, and, after a very severe conflict, obliged Lieut.-Colonel Floyd to fall back. The troops from Coimbatore, however, had marched to his support, and, on the junction being effected, Tippoo Saïb retired. The British returned to

1790. Coimbatore on the 23rd September. Upon the march of the main body, the flank companies of the Seventy-first and Seventy-second were withdrawn from the siege of Palghautcherry, and ordered to take post in the fort of Coimbatore: and on the return of the army they rejoined their regiments.

The army was again put in motion on the 29th September, proceeding towards the Boovany by Shawoor and Coopachittypollum, where the troops arrived a few hours after Tippoo Saïb had left it. Some elephants, bullocks, and camels, loaded with rockets, fell into the hands of the British. On the 4th of October the army arrived at Errode, the enemy keeping a respectful distance during the march, and on the 6th it was ascertained that he had arrived with his entire force at Darraporam, against which he opened his batteries on the 8th. The fort had no cannon mounted, and the garrison, consisting of 100 Europeans and 200 Sepoys, capitulated on honourable terms, which were strictly adhered to. The British army moved on the 5th October, and on the 15th encamped in the neighbourhood of Coimbatore, where Lieut.-Colonel Stuart joined from Palghautcherry, after having taken that place, and left it in a tolerable state of defence. On the 20th October, all the heavy baggage having been deposited in the fort of Coimbatore, the army marched towards Errode, by Avinochy and Perentore, where it arrived on the 2nd November. On the 8th the army proceeded in the direction of Bovancore, and thence to a ford about three miles below Errode, the whole crossing the Cavery on the 9th and 10th, while Tippoo Saïb moved his entire force against a division under the orders of Lieut.-Colonel Maxwell, Seventy-fourth Regiment, then in the Bharamahl country. On the 11th November the army moved by Saukerrydroog on the Tappoor Pass, and ascended on the 14th, encamping at Adomancettah in the Bharamahl country: it marched again on the 15th, and effected its junction with Lieut.-Colonel Maxwell at Darampoury on the 17th. The whole force was now divided into ten brigades. The Seventy-fourth Highlanders joined the Seventy-first and Seventy-second in the Second Brigade; and Lieut.-Colonel Maxwell assumed command of the left wing in place of Colonel Brydges, who was appointed to command at Trichinopoly.

It was now ascertained that the enemy, whose movements were always sudden, varied, and perplexing, was directing his course to the Carnatic by Namacul and Trichinopoly. The British, in consequence, pursued by Malusundrum, arriving on the 23rd at Vavoor, the 27th at Jaloor, the 6th December at Munsarapett, at Terany on the last day of the year, and the 12th January, 1791, at Arnee. During this long and fatiguing march, the Anglo-Indian troops frequently encamped upon the ground from which the enemy had removed in the morning, but the efforts made to overtake him were unsuccessful. The heavy guns and the sick having been left in the fort of Arnee, the army proceeded to Velhout, where on the 29th January it was reviewed by General Charles the Earl Cornwallis, K.G., who had arrived from Bengal to assume command, and who expressed great satisfaction at the appearance of the troops. His Lordship was at this period Governor-General and Commander-in-Chief in the East Indies. In the course of the foregoing campaign the Seventy-first lost few men in action, but many fell victims to climate and fatigue.

The army, being refreshed and equipped, commenced moving in a westerly direction on the 5th February, and passing by Perambaukum and Sholingar, arrived on the 11th in the vicinity of Vellore. On the 14th it marched by Chittipet and Chittoor towards the Muglee Pass, which it reached on the 17th. The following day the advance, followed by the park and stores, ascended the Ghauts, the whole army

margin notes: 1730. 1791.

1791. encamping on the 19th at Palamnaire, in the Mysore country, without having seen anything of the enemy. During the time the British army remained at Velhout Tippoo Saïb pushed southward and summoned Cuddalore, but upon hearing in what direction Earl Cornwallis had moved the Sultan hastened to the Shangana Pass, where he arrived too late to oppose the troops at the Muglee Pass. On the 24th the British marched to Colar, which was abandoned on their approach, and the army moved on to Ouscotta, which was carried by a battalion of sepoys. The enemy displayed a part of his force on the 4th March, and on the following day opened a cannonade upon the troops moving towards Bangalore, whilst his horse attempted to seize the stores and baggage, but without success. About sunset on the 5th March the army encamped within shot of the fort of Bangalore. The day following the suburbs of the town were attacked by the Thirty-sixth and Seventy-sixth Regiments, with some battalions of sepoys, and carried after a very resolute resistance on the part of the defenders. From this period to the 14th March nothing material occurred, but every preparation for the approaching siege was carried on with diligence and activity. On the 15th, the batteries being completed, opened fire upon Bangalore, and on the 17th the lines were cannonaded by the enemy, while at night the camp was much disturbed by his rockets. Forage became very scarce, and none could be procured beyond the advanced pickets. The siege, however, proceeded, the enemy continuing to harass the besiegers until the 21st March, when the breach being considered practicable, an attack was ordered. The storming party consisted of the grenadiers of the European regiments, followed by their light companies, and led by Lieutenant James Duncan, Seventy-first Highlanders, and Lieutenant John Evans, Fifty-second Regiment, with a forlorn hope of thirty chosen men, the whole supported by the battalion companies of the Thirty-sixth, Seventy-second, and Seventy-sixth Regiments, with some battalions of Bengal sepoys. The attacking force was commanded by Lieut.-Colonel Maxwell, Seventy-fourth Highlanders, the flankers by Major Kelly; Major-General Meadows was present on the occasion. The grenadier company, Seventy-first Highlanders, was commanded by Captain the Honourable John Lindsay, who, upon entering the breach, directed his men to throw away their priming and trust entirely to their bayonets. The light company was commanded by Captain James Robertson, son of the celebrated historian. With the aid of scaling ladders, and after encountering very formidable obstacles, Bangalore was carried. From the 6th March to the capture of Bangalore the Seventy-first had 6 privates killed and 14 wounded. On the 28th March, a strong garrison being left in Bangalore, the army moved to Deonhully, the birthplace of Hyder Ali, where it arrived on the 30th, and on the 1st April at Chinnaballaporam, both of which places were abandoned by the enemy. The army reached Connapelly on the 12th April, and on the following day effected a junction with the Nizam's force, which had been sent to co-operate with the British, and which amounted to about 15,000 cavalry. On the 18th April the army arrived at Venkatagherry, where a large detachment of Europeans, under Colonel Oldham, joined from the Carnatic, and on the 22nd April it again encamped near Bangalore. During this march, the object of which was chiefly to secure supplies, the enemy's irregular horse were now and then seen in small detached bodies. On the 4th May the army marched towards Seringapatam, the capital of Tippoo Saïb's territory, and on the 13th reached Arakerry, on the Cavery, about eight miles below Seringapatam. The enemy could be seen in front, with their right resting on the river, and their left on a high hill named the Carig-

1791.

1791. haut. During the night of the 14th of May the troops marched with a view to surprising the enemy, but owing to the badness of the weather and roads, together with the jaded state of the gun bullocks, little or no progress was made during the night, but on the following day, after undergoing great fatigue, they were brought into action. The enemy was then soon driven from his strong position, and forced across the river to the island upon which the capital, Seringapatam, is situated, where he was protected by his batteries. In this affair four guns and several standards were taken. The Seventy-first lost Lieutenant and Adjutant Roderick Mackenzie and 7 rank and file killed. Ensign John Stuart and 74 rank and file were wounded. The army rested upon the field of battle, and moving again on the 18th arrived at Canambaddy, on the Cavery, upon the 20th. It was now ascertained that the season was too far advanced for undertaking immediately the siege of Tippoo Saīb's capital, and it was determined accordingly to withdraw. The battering train was destroyed, all the ammunition stores which could not be removed were buried, and on the 26th May the army marched in the direction of Bangalore. In the course of this retreat the British were joined by the Mahratta army, consisting of about 33,000 men, chiefly cavalry, and 30 pieces of cannon. Of the approach of this large force the British had been kept in total ignorance by the activity of Tippoo's irregular troops. Captain Little, with two battalions of Bombay sepoys, joined with the Mahratta army, and supplies were now abundant.

On the 11th July the army arrived at Bangalore without any attempt on the part of the enemy to interrupt the march. By this time the Nizam's cavalry had become unfit to keep the field, and were allowed to return to their own country. A large detachment of the Mahrattas proceeded into the Sera country, the remainder continuing with the British army. On the 15th July the sick and 1791. half of the tumbrils belonging to the field pieces were sent into the fort of Bangalore, and the army moved towards Oussoor, where it arrived on the 11th of the following month. The fort of Oussoor was abandoned by the enemy after he had blown up the angles.

On the 12th of August the army moved from Oussoor, and on the 23rd arrived at Bayeur. About this period Major Gowdie, of the Honourable East India Company's Service, was detached with some troops for the reduction of the strong hill fort of Nundydroog, which it was found required regular approaches. The flank companies of the Thirty-sixth and Seventy-first Regiments, under the command of Captain Robertson of the latter corps, marched on the 17th of October to join the detachment under Major Gowdie, and, upon their arrival, were immediately placed in the last parallel.

On the 18th of October General the Earl Cornwallis with the whole army, made a movement towards Nundydroog, and in the evening of that day the troops were told off for an assault upon the two breaches, which had been pronounced practicable. The attacks commenced at eleven o'clock at night, the grenadiers assaulting the right breach and the light companies the left. The forlorn hope of the right attack consisted of twenty grenadiers, volunteers from the Thirty-sixth and Seventy-first, led by Lieutenant Hugh Mackenzie of the Seventy-first, afterwards for a long time paymaster of the regiment. The same number of light infantry, headed by Lieutenant Lewis Moore, of the Seventy-first, formed the left attack. The grenadier company of the regiment, in support, was commanded by Lieutenant James Duncan, the light company by Lieutenant Kenneth Mackenzie, the whole under Captain Robertson's orders. Captain Robert Burne supported, with the Thirty-sixth grenadiers, the right attack, and

1791. Captain William Hartley, with the light company of that regiment, the left attack; Major-General Meadows, as usual, animating the whole with his presence. Both breaches were carried without much resistance from the enemy, and the gateway of the inner wall being soon secured, the fort fell into the possession of the British. Many of the enemy were killed, and several, in attempting to escape, were dashed to pieces over the precipices. It was an additional source of gratification that this important service had been achieved without the loss of a British soldier. The following general order was issued on this occasion:—

"*Head Quarters Camp, October* 20*th*, 1791.

" Lord Cornwallis having been witness of the extra-
" ordinary obstacles, both of nature and art, which were
" opposed to the detachment of the army that attacked
" Nundydroog, he cannot too highly applaud the firmness
" and exertions which were manifested by all ranks in car-
" rying on the operations of the siege, or the valour and
" discipline which were displayed by the flank companies
" of His Majesty's Thirty-sixth and Seventy-first Regi-
" ments (other regiments of native infantry were here
" enumerated) that were employed in the assault last night,
" and which, by overcoming all difficulties, effected the re-
" duction of that important fort, and he particularly desires
" that his warmest thanks may be presented to Captain
" Robertson of the Seventy-first Regiment, who com-
" manded the flank companies that led the assaults."

In a few days subsequently to the fall of Nundydroog the army retraced its route to Bangalore. On the 4th of December the troops were again put in movement, directing their march towards Savendroog, a fortress situated on the side of a mountain surrounded by almost inaccessible rocks. The fort being reconnoitred, a detachment, under

Lieut.-Colonel James Stuart of the Seventy-second Regi- 1791.
ment, was selected and ordered to reduce the place. On
the 17th the British were enabled to open upon the fort a
battery of six 18-pounders and three 12-pounders with
considerable effect. The flank companies of the Seventy-
first and Seventy-sixth Regiments joined the detachment
under Lieut.-Colonel Stuart on the 20th of December, and
on the following day the flank companies of the Fifty-
second, Seventy-first, Seventy-second, and Seventy-sixth
were selected for the attack upon Savendroog, in which a
practicable breach had been effected, and formed under
Lieut.-Colonel Colebrook Nesbitt, of the Fifty-second
Regiment. The storming party, commanded by Lieut.-
Colonel Nesbitt, was directed to four different attacks:
Captain James Gage, with the grenadiers of the Fifty-
second and flank companies of the Seventy-sixth Regiments, to gain the eastern hill to the left; Captain the
Hon. John Lindsay and Captain James Robertson, with
the flank companies of the Seventy-first, to separate and
attack the works or parties they might discover in the
chasm or hollow between the hills; the Fifty-second and
Seventy-second Regiments were to follow the flank companies. Parties were detached under Lieut.-Colonel Baird
and Major Petrie round the mountain to draw the attention of the enemy from the main object, and to endeavour
to prevent his escape. At eleven o'clock in the morning
of the 21st of December, on a signal of two guns being
fired from the batteries, the flank companies, in the order
described, followed by the Fifty-second and Seventy-
second Regiments, advanced to the assaults, the band of
the Fifty-second playing "Britons, strike home," while the
grenadiers and light infantry mounted the breach. Immediate success followed the attempt, the fort being carried
without the loss of a man. The troops were thanked in
general orders for their gallànt conduct, as follows:—

1791. "Lord Cornwallis thinks himself fortunate, almost beyond example, in having acquired by assault a fortress of so much strength and reputation, and of such inestimable value to the public interest as Savendroog, without having to regret the loss of a single soldier. . . .

"Although the resistance was so contemptible, he is not the less sensible that the behaviour of the grenadiers and light infantry of the Fifty-second, Seventy-first, Seventy-second, and Seventy-sixth Regiments, who led the assaults, and who must have made the decisive impression upon the minds of the enemy, reflects the most distinguished honour upon their discipline and valour."

Outredroog, Ram Gurry, and Sheria Gurry shortly afterwards surrendered to the British Army. The force subsequently moved towards Outredroog, a hill fort about thirty miles west of Bangalore, where a general hospital

1792. was established. On the 31st of January, 1792, the army, under General the Earl Cornwallis, was reviewed by the Poonah and Hyderabad Chiefs, and on the following day commenced its march towards Seringapatam, passing by Hooleadroog, Tagilly, and Carrycode. The troops came in sight of Tippoo's capital on the 3rd of February, and encamped at the French Rocks. The enemy's horse showed itself on the 4th and 5th, but attempted nothing hostile.

The entrenched camp of Tippoo Saïb was reconnoitred on the 6th of February, and at dark the army was formed in three columns of attack. The right, under Major-General Meadows, consisting of the Thirty-sixth and Seventy-sixth King's Regiments ; the centre, under the Commander-in-Chief, General the Earl Cornwallis, consisting of the Fifty-second, Seventy-first, and Seventy-fourth King's Regiments. The left, under Lieut.-Colonel Maxwell, of the Seventy-fourth, was composed of the Seventy-second Regiment. The native troops were divided among the three columns.

By eight o'clock in the evening of the 6th of February, the 1792. three columns were in motion. The head of the centre column, led by the flank companies of the respective corps, after twice crossing the Sohany river, which covered the enemy's right wing and front, came in contact with his first line, and immediately forced its way through it. The British flankers, mixing with the fugitives, crossed the north branch of the Cavery, at the foot of the glacis of the fort of Seringapatam. Captain the Honourable John Lindsay collected the grenadiers of the Seventy-first upon the glacis, and attempted to push into the body of the place, but was prevented by the bridge being raised a few moments before he reached it. He was soon after joined by some of the light company of the Fifty-second and grenadiers of the Seventy-sixth, with whom he forced his way down to the famous "Lal bagh," or Ruby Garden, where he was attacked most furiously, but the enemy was repelled with the bayonet.

Captain Lindsay was afterwards joined by the Seventy-fourth grenadiers, and attempted to drive the enemy from the Pettah, but could not succeed, from the numbers which poured on him from all sides. This gallant officer then took post in a redoubt, where he maintained himself until morning, and then moved to the north bank of the river, where the firing appeared very heavy. He was there met by Brevet Lieutenant-Colonel the Honourable John Knox, of the Thirty-sixth Regiment, and by Lieut.-Colonel Baird, with the grenadiers of the Fifty-second and the light company of the Seventy-first, together with some of the troops that composed the left attack.

During these occurrences the battalion companies of the Fifty-second, Seventy-first, and Seventy-second Regiments forced their way across the river to the island, over-powering all that opposed them, when Captain Archdeacon, commanding a battalion of Bengal sepoys, being killed,

1792. that battalion was thrown into confusion, falling back upon the Seventy-first. Major Stair Park Dalrymple, wishing to prevent the sepoys intermingling with his men, ordered the regiment to move obliquely to the left, an operation that by chance brought him in contact with the Sultan's redoubt, which was instantly attacked and carried. The charge of the redoubt was given to Captain Hugh Sibbald, of the Seventy-first, with his company, who on the following morning was killed, nobly defending it against repeated and desperate attacks from the enemy. He was replaced by Major Shelly, under whom the redoubt sustained two serious assaults. The Commander-in-Chief, General the Earl Cornwallis, in compliment to the memory of this officer, had the name of the redoubt changed to "Sibbald."

In the evening of the 7th of February 3,000 of the enemy's horse attacked the British troops on the island, but were repulsed by the Seventy-first Regiment and the First Coast Sepoys. In the course of these operations the regiment had Captain Sibbald and Lieutenant Daniel Bayne killed; Ensign Duncan Mackenzie was wounded; about 100 rank and file were killed and wounded.

The enemy's loss was very severe, being estimated at 20,000 *hors de combat*. Eighty pieces of cannon were taken by the British. The following general order was issued:—

"Feb. 7th.

"'The conduct and valour of the officers and soldiers of
" this army have often merited Lord Cornwallis's enco-
" miums, but the zeal and gallantry which were so success-
" fully displayed last night in the attacks of the enemy's
" whole army in a position which had cost him so much
" time and labour to fortify, can never be sufficiently
" praised; and his satisfaction on an occasion which pro-
" mised to be attended with the most substantial advan-
" tages has been greatly heightened by learning from the

"commanding officers of divisions that this meritorious 1792.
"behaviour was universal through all ranks, to a degree
"that has been rarely equalled. Lord Cornwallis there-
"fore requests that the army in general will accept of his
"most cordial thanks for the noble and gallant manner in
"which they have executed the plan of the attack; it
"covers them with honour, and will ever command his
"warmest sentiments of admiration."

On the 9th of February the army took up its final position for the siege of Seringapatam, and on the 15th Major-General Robert Abercromby joined with the Bombay force, consisting of the Seventy-third, Seventy-fifth, and Seventy-seventh regiments, besides native troops, making a total of about 6,000 men.

The Seventy-first Highlanders, commanded by Major Dalrymple, crossed the south branch of the Cavery at nine o'clock at night on the 18th of February, and two hours later attacked by surprise a camp of the enemy's cavalry, of whom a great part were slain and the remainder dispersed in all directions. This movement was designed to cover the operation of opening the trenches, which took place at the same time within 800 yards of the fort. Until the 24th of February the approaches were carried on with the greatest activity, when the general orders announced that the preliminary articles of peace had been signed, and in consequence all hostile measures immediately ceased.

On the 26th of February the two sons of Tippoo Saïb, Abd-el-Khalik and Musa-ed-Deen, the former ten years of age and the latter eight, were brought to the British camp as hostages for the due performance of the preliminary articles.

In consequence of some obstacles which had been opposed by Tippoo to the arrangement of the definitive treaty, working parties were ordered, and the guns replaced in the batteries on the 10th March. This state of suspicion

1792. and preparation lasted until the 15th of March, when it was discontinued, and on the 18th of that month, the definitive treaty being duly executed and signed, was delivered by the young Abd-el-Khalik to each of the confederates. On the 20th the counterpart was sent to Tippoo Saïb.

Thus terminated a war in which the confederates wrested from the enemy 70 fortresses, 800 pieces of cannon, and destroyed or dispersed at least 50,000 men. By the articles of the treaty Tippoo Saïb was bound to pay a large sum of money and to cede one-half of his dominions. The Governor-General and Commander-in-Chief in India granted from this money a sum equal to six months' batta for all ranks, and the Court of Directors afterwards made a similar grant. The East India Company also granted an annuity of £50 to Captain P. Melville for his services in India.

On the 26th of March, the exchange of the definitive treaty being completed, the British commenced moving towards Bangalore, from whence they proceeded to the Pednaigdurgum Pass, where the Bengal troops were ordered to their own Presidency.

Early in May the army descended the Ghauts, arriving soon after at Vellore, where the Commander-in-Chief arranged the cantonments of the troops and proceeded to Madras. The Seventy-first received orders to march to the southward, and in the month of June arrived at Warriore, near Trichinopoly, under the command of Lieut.-Colonel Baird, who during the campaign had been absent from the regiment in command of a brigade. Eight companies were stationed at Warriore, and two were detached with Major Dalrymple to Dindigul. In this situation the regiment continued for the remainder of the year.

1793. In March, 1793, the eight companies under the command of Lieut.-Colonel Baird proceeded from Warriore to

Secundermally, in the neighbourhood of Madura. Mean- 1793. while the events of the French Revolution had involved England in another contest, the National Convention of France having declared war against Great Britain and Holland in February, 1793. The news of this event arrived in India in May following, when the siege of the French settlement of Pondicherry, on the Coromandel coast, was determined upon. Lieut.-Colonel Baird, of the Seventy-first, was appointed to command a brigade on this service.

In July the flank companies of the regiment were ordered to join the force about to besiege Pondicherry, and marched for that purpose, being followed soon afterwards by the battalion companies. The place surrendered on the 22nd of August, and the Seventy-first returned to Secundermally and Dindigul, where it continued during the remainder of the year.

An attack upon the Mauritius was in contemplation at 1794. the commencement of the year 1794, and troops for that service were assembled at Wallajohabad. The Seventy-first, having received orders to join this force, marched to Wallajohabad, where the regiment remained only a short time, having been ordered to return to the southward, in consequence of the projected expedition being relinquished.

The regiment marched accordingly, and arrived at Tanjore in June, where it was stationed for the remainder of the year, having two companies detached under Major Dalrymple at Vellum.

Holland became united to France in the early part of 1795. 1795, and was styled the Batavian Republic. Upon the arrival of this information in India, an expedition was fitted out against the Island of Ceylon, where the Dutch had several settlements. Major Dalrymple, with the flank companies, marched to the coast, and embarked at Nega-

1795. patam, for the purpose of co-operating with the troops destined for Ceylon, under the command of Colonel James Stuart, of the Seventy-second, who was promoted to the rank of Major-General at this period. The fleet arrived on the coast of Ceylon on the 1st of August, and two days afterwards the troops landed four miles north of the fort of Trincomalee. The siege of the fort was commenced as soon as the artillery and stores could be landed and removed sufficiently near to the place. On the 26th of August a practicable breach was effected, and the garrison surrendered. The fort of Batticaloe surrendered on the 18th of September, and the fort and island of Manaar capitulated on the 5th of October. After these services were performed, the flank companies returned to Tanjore in the month of October, having lost 11 men in killed and wounded. Captain William Charles Gorrie, of the grenadier company, was desperately wounded in this expedition.

The following honourable mention of an officer in this regiment is extracted from a letter of Sir Robert Abercromby to the Duke of York.

"*Calcutta, November 4th.*

"I have the honour to inform you that Major Dirom
" having resigned his office of Deputy Adjutant-General in
" India, I have appointed Captain James Robertson, of the
" Seventy-first Regiment, who has acted for him since 1st
" July, 1792, to succeed until His Majesty's pleasure is
" known, as Captain Robertson was included in the brevet
" of Major, made in March, 1794, though not yet published
" in India, and I am sensible any further mark of His
" Majesty's favour will be pleasing to the Marquis Cornwallis, under whom he served, and I beg leave to recommend him for the rank of Lieut.-Colonel."

1796. In May, 1796, the regiment marched to Wallajohabad, where it was stationed during the remainder of the year.

On the 2nd of January, 1797, the regiment was inspected by Major-General Clarke, who issued the following general order:—

"Major-General Clarke has experienced infinite satis-
"faction this morning at the review of His Majesty's
"Seventy-first Regiment.

"He cannot say that on any occasion of field exercise
"he ever was present at a more perfect performance.

"When a corps is so striking in appearance, and so
"complete in every branch of its discipline, little can occur
"to the Commander-in-Chief to particularize. He cannot
"but notice, however, that the Seventy-first Regiment has
"excited his admiration for its expertness in those parts
"of its exercise which are most essential and most difficult
"to execute. He alludes to its order and regularity when
"moving in line, its extreme accuracy in preserving dis-
"tance, and the neatness and promptitude that are so
"evident in all its formations. So much perfection in a
"corps whose services in India will long be held in remem-
"brance, does the greatest honour to Lieut.-Colonel Baird
"and all his officers, to whom and the corps at large the
"Commander-in-Chief desires to offer his best thanks."

The regiment remained in the cantonment of Wallajo-habad until the month of October, when orders were issued for its return to Europe. It was accordingly drafted, giving five hundred men to the Seventy-third and Seventy-fourth Regiments, and then marched from Wallajohabad, under the command of Colonel Baird, to Madras, and immediately embarked on board of Indiamen for Great Britain. The fleet sailed from Madras Roads on the 17th of October, and was at sea during the remainder of the year. A few days previous to its embarkation the following order was published:—

1797.

"*Fort St. George,*
"*October* 16*th*, 1797.

" General Order by Government.

" The officers, non-commissioned officers, drummers,
" and privates of the Seventy-first Highlanders are under
" orders for Europe, to embark to-morrow morning at six.
" The President in Council has much satisfaction in ex-
" pressing the great sense entertained by the Government
" of the active, zealous, and important services of the
" Seventy-first Highlanders during the eighteen years they
" have been stationed in India, by which they have con-
" tributed so largely to the reputation of the British Army,
" and so essentially promoted the interests of the East
" India Company.

" By order of the Right Honourable the President in
" Council.

(Signed) " S. WEBBE,
" *Secretary to the Government.*"

This high testimonial of the approbation of the Civil Government was accompanied by the following mark of commendation from the Commander-in-Chief:—

" General Order by Lieut.-General Harris.

" The Commander-in-Chief cannot think of parting
" with a corps that has been so eminently distinguished
" as the Seventy-first Highlanders in India by a series of
" long, arduous, and spirited services, without requesting
" Lieut.-Colonel Baird, the officers, non-commissioned
" officers, and every man belonging to that regiment to
" accept of his warmest acknowledgments for conduct
" which has been equally honourable to them, and advan-
" tageous to their country. The alacrity with which
" Lieut.-Colonel Baird has arranged, at a short warning,
" everything relative to the drafting, confirms Lieutenant-

"General Harris in the favourable opinion he had formed 1797.
"of the internal order and discipline of that corps, and he
"trusts that the regularity and zeal of the men destined
"for the Seventy-third and Seventy-fourth Highlanders
"will be such as to maintain the high reputation they have
"so deservedly acquired.
   (Signed) ". J. ROBERTSON,
        "*Deputy Adjutant-General.*
"*Head-Quarters, Choultry Plain,*
 "*October* 16*th*, 1797."

Early in January, 1798, the fleet arrived at the Cape 1798.
of Good Hope, where the commanding officer of the regiment, Colonel Baird, was detained upon the Staff, having been appointed Brigadier-General. After remaining a few days in Table Bay, the fleet sailed, and reached St. Helena in February, where it was detained three months, waiting for a convoy.

The fleet sailed on the 1st of May from St. Helena, without a convoy, and in July, in consequence of contrary winds, was compelled to put into Cork Harbour. It sailed from thence for the Thames, and on the 13th of August the regiment disembarked at Woolwich, where it remained for a few days, and then re-embarked in smacks for Leith. After landing, the regiment proceeded to Stirling. As a mark of indulgence, a general leave for two months was granted to the officers and men of the Seventy-first, to enable them to visit their friends and families after the long absence from their native country. At the expiration of this period, the whole assembled at Stirling, with the addition of a few recruits.* Immediately afterwards, the

---

* On the 23rd of May, 1821, His Majesty King George IV was graciously pleased to authorise the Seventy-first to bear on the regimental colours and appointments the word "Hindoostan," in commemoration of its distinguished services in the several actions in which it had been engaged, while in India, between the years 1780 and 1797.

1798. whole of the officers and non-commissioned officers, with the exception of the Staff, and a few at head-quarters, were sent out to recruit for the regiment.

Very few of the men remained who had originally formed the regiment; of the officers, the following were still in the regiment :—

>Colonel Baird,
>   „   Dalrymple,
>Major Lindsay Robertson,
>Brevet-Major Borthwick,
>   „   Gorrie,
>Captain D. Ross,
>   „   Hugh Cuthbert,
>   „   Roderick McKenzie,
>   „   Hugh McKenzie.

1799. During the year 1799, the head-quarters remained at Stirling, and the recruiting went on but slowly.

1800. In May, 1800, the strength of the regiment amounted to about 200 rank and file, when a route arrived changing the quarters to Paisley, but soon after the march an order arrived for its proceeding to Ireland. In June the regiment reached Portpatrick, and crossed immediately to Donaghadee, from whence it marched, under the command of Colonel Dalrymple, to Newry, and in a few days afterwards was removed to Dundalk.

In July the regiment received 600 volunteers from the Scotch Fencible Corps serving in Ireland, and remained at Dundalk until the close of the year, when a route for Dublin was received. At this period, Colonel Dalrymple was appointed Brigadier-General, and the command of the regiment devolved on Brevet Lieut.-Colonel John French.

On the 6th of December Major Denis Pack was promoted from the Fourth Royal Irish Dragoon Guards to be

Lieut.-Colonel in the Seventy-first Regiment, in succession 1800. to Lieut.-Colonel the Honourable John Lindsay, who retired from the service.

The regiment, early in the year 1801, marched from 1801. Dundalk to Dublin, and occupied the barracks in the Palatine Square. On the 24th of April, Lieut.-Colonel Pack joined, and assumed the command of the regiment.

In March, 1802, in which month the Peace of Amiens 1802. was concluded, the regiment proceeded from Dublin, and was quartered in the county of Wicklow. The corps was so divided, that at Arklow, the head-quarters, there were only two companies. In this situation it continued for the remainder of the year.

The regiment proceeded in March, 1803, in three divi- 1803. sions, to Ballinasloe, where it remained for a few days, and afterwards marched to Loughrea.

Major-General Sir John Francis Cradock, K.B., was appointed Colonel of the Seventy-first Highlanders on the 6th of August, 1803, in succession to General the Honourable William Gordon, who was removed to the Twenty-first Royal North British Fusiliers.

The regiment continued at Loughrea, but the light company was detached to Limerick to join a light battalion which was being formed at that place. Captain Sinclair died during this year, and the officers of the regiment caused a stone to be erected over his grave bearing the following inscription:—

" To the memory of Captain John Sinclair, this stone
" was caused to be placed by his brother officers of the
" Seventy-first Regiment, as a testimony of the high esteem
" they held him in as an officer, as well as the sincere love
" they bore him as a friend. Twenty-six years spent in
" zealous and faithful discharge of his duty justly entitled
" him to the character of the one, and the many estimable
" qualities of the heart gave him no less claim to the

D 2

1803. "other; he died at the age of 41, in the year of our Lord "1803, resigning only with his breath that commission "which His Gracious Majesty had pleased to bestow."

1804. In May the regiment proceeded from Loughrea to the county of Limerick; the head-quarters being stationed at Rathkeale, one detachment at Newcastle, another at Tarbert, and a third at Askeaton.

2nd bat. While the regiment was stationed in Ireland, war had recommenced with France, and Bonaparte having made preparations for invading Great Britain, additional measures of defence to those of the former year were adopted by the Government; and under the "*Additional Force Act*," passed on the 10th of July, 1804, a second battalion was added to the Seventy-first Regiment, which was to consist of men to be raised for limited service in certain counties of North Britain. The second battalion was formed at Dumbarton in October, to the command of which Lieut.-Colonel Lord George Beresford was appointed. Its establishment was fixed at 23 sergeants, 22 drummers, 20 corporals, 1,380 privates.

1805. In March, 1805, the first battalion, under the command 1st bat. of Lieut.-Colonel Pack, proceeded to Bandon, in the county of Cork, and was stationed at that place until July, when it marched to Cork, and immediately afterwards to Monkstown, where it embarked in transports, having been selected to form part of a secret expedition under its former commander, Major-General Sir David Baird.

In the beginning of August the embarkation was completed, and on the 5th of that month the fleet sailed, convoyed by three 64-gun ships, two frigates and gun brigs, under the orders of Commodore Sir Home Popham; and on the 28th of September the fleet, after a very boisterous passage, arrived at Madeira.

On the 3rd of October the fleet left Madeira, and on the 12th of November arrived at St. Salvador, in the

Brazils, where an opportunity was afforded of refreshing 1805. the men, landing the sick, and procuring some horses for the cavalry.

The fleet again put to sea on the 28th of November, and directed its course towards the Dutch Colony of the Cape of Good Hope, then in possession of the Batavian Government, which was united with France in hostility to Great Britain.

It arrived at the high table-land of the Cape of Good 1806. Hope on the 4th of January, 1806, and shortly afterwards came to anchor. The whole of the following day the surf upon the shore of the bay was too violent to admit of any attempt to land. Brigadier-General William Carr, afterwards General Viscount Beresford, was detached, with such of the cavalry as had horses, and the Thirty-eighth Regiment, to Saldanha Bay.

In the morning of the 6th of January a landing was effected by the Highland brigade, consisting of the Seventy-first, Seventy-second, and Ninety-third Highlanders, and numbering 2,200 men, under the command of Brigadier-General Ronald Craufurd Ferguson, in the performance of which service Lieut.-Colonel Pack, the commanding officer of the Seventy-first Regiment, was wounded. The following day was devoted to landing the supplies and the remainder of the army.

Early in the morning of the 8th of January, Major-General Sir David Baird formed his troops in two columns, and moved up to the heights of Bleuberg, from whence the enemy was seen, drawn up in order of battle, in two lines, with twenty-three pieces of cannon, his numbers being calculated at 5,000, of which a large proportion was cavalry.

The British lines were formed with promptitude and correctness, and the enemy was attacked with the utmost spirit. He maintained his ground with some firmness, until

1806. a charge of the Highland brigade dislodged and completely routed him, with the loss of three guns and 700 men.

In this affair the Seventy-first had Brevet Lieut.-Colonel Robert Campbell wounded. 5 men were killed, and 2 sergeants and 64 rank and file were wounded.*

The troops halted for the night at the Reit Valley, and on the 9th of January the army moved towards the Salt River, where it was intended to take up a position previously to the attack of Cape Town, when a flag of truce appeared from the town, which produced some negociations, that terminated in its surrender to His Majesty's arms. Lieut.-General Janssens, the Governor of the colony, after his defeat of Blenberg on the 8th, had retired towards the interior of the country by the Hottentot Holland Kloof, or Pass, from whence, on the 19th of January, he signed and ratified the treaty that placed the whole of the Cape of Good Hope and its dependencies in the possession of Great Britain, under whose sway it has since continued.

1st bat. The following letter from Brigadier-General Ferguson to Major-General Sir David Baird, relative to the regiment and its commander, is here inserted :—

" Sir,   "*Cape Town*, 19*th January*, 1806.

" As in the affair of Bleuberg, on the 8th instant,
" chance placed two of the enemy's guns in possession of
" the Highland brigade, I hope you will be pleased to
" order the allowance usually granted on such occasions
" to be issued and shared amongst the Seventy-first,
" Seventy-second, and Ninety-third Regiments.

" Although the guns fell into our hands in front of the
„ Seventy-first Highlanders, Lieut.-Colonel Pack (desirous

---

* The royal authority was subsequently granted for the Seventy-first to bear the words "Cape of Good Hope" on the regimental colours and appointments, to commemorate its distinguished gallantry at the capture of that colony.

"that the three regiments should be considered as one
" family) has most handsomely withdrawn the prior claim
" His Majesty's Seventy-first Highlanders might have
" made, and to which the situation of the guns, when
" taken, would have entitled that most excellent corps.

1806.
1st bat.

"I have, etc.,
(Signed) "R. C. FERGUSON,
"*Brigadier-General.*
"*Major-General Sir David Baird.*"

The Seventy-first went into quarters at the cantonment of Wynberg, about seven miles from Cape Town, on the road to Simon's Bay, where the battalion remained until the 12th of April, when, most unexpectedly, an order arrived for its immediate embarkation on an expedition to the Rio de la Plata, in South America, which had been planned by the British Commanders, naval and military, at the Cape. The Seventy-first was the only corps of the Cape garrison destined for this service, with the addition of a few dragoons and some artillery. At this period the strength of the battalion amounted to 800 rank and file, having received some recruits from foreign corps at the Cape. The troops were to be commanded by Brigadier-General William Carr Beresford, afterwards Viscount Beresford.

The battalion was embarked in line-of-battle ships and transports, and on the 14th of April the fleet sailed from Table Bay, directing its course to the westward until the 20th, when, in consequence of unfavourable weather, and having parted company with one of the transports in which were three companies of the Seventy-first, the signal was made to rendezvous at St. Helena, at which island the fleet arrived on the 30th of April, with the exception of the missing transport. Here the force under Brigadier-General Beresford received an augmentation of 200 men

1806. from the St. Helena Regiment, making a total of 1,087 rank and file.
1st bat.

On the 2nd of May the fleet sailed from St. Helena, and after a tedious voyage arrived at Cape St. Mary at the entrance of the Rio de la Plata, on the 8th of June, where it met with the missing transport.

The troops that had sailed in the line-of-battle ships were transferred on the 16th of June to the transports, which proceeded up the river, and on the 24th of that month came to anchor opposite the city of Buenos Ayres. The force amounted in all to 1,466 rank and file; the Seventy-first mustered 784 rank and file. On the 25th, at night, the Seventy-first, with the other troops, effected a landing without any opposition. The following morning they pushed forward, and met the enemy at the village of Reduccion, who made a trifling stand, and then retired towards the city. On this occasion Captain Henry Le Blanc of the Seventy-first lost his leg, and a sergeant and 5 rank and file were wounded.

The British troops continued to advance in pursuit of the enemy, and on the morning of the 27th of June forced their passage across the Rio Chuelo. Some skirmishing followed this movement, but the city of Buenos Ayres almost immediately surrendered. In the evening the town and fort were taken possession of by the first battalion of the Seventy-first and detachments of marines and St. Helena Regiment. Major-General Beresford, in his despatch to Sir David Baird, wrote as follows:—

"I cannot omit reporting to you that I had the most just cause to be satisfied with the conduct of every officer and all the troops under my command; to Lieut.-Colonel Pack, of the Seventy-first Highlanders, every praise is due, as well as to that excellent regiment."

The Seventy-first occupied barracks in Buenos Ayres, and remained undisturbed until the beginning of August, by which time the enemy had collected a force of about 1,500 men, under a leader named Pueridon, at five leagues from the city. Brigadier-General Beresford in consequence moved out with 300 of the Seventy-first, 50 from the St. Helena Regiment, and six field pieces; attacked and dispersed the enemy, taking all his artillery, namely, ten pieces of various calibre. The battalion had only 5 men wounded in this operation.

1806. 1st bat.

About this period a body of the enemy, headed by Colonel Liniers, a French officer in the service of Spain, crossed from Colonna to Concher, evidently with hostile intentions. Forming a junction with the force under Pueridon, the whole marched upon Buenos Ayres.

On the 10th of August the enemy commenced operations by the massacre of a sergeant and his guard of the Seventy-first Regiment, who were posted at a place in the suburbs where the bull-fights were usually exhibited. On the following day much skirmishing ensued in the outskirts of the city, the enemy taking possession of the tops of houses, from which he kept up a galling and destructive fire. During this time the main body of the British force took up a position in the Grand Square, but afterwards retired into the fort of Buenos Ayres. Being now bereft of all resources, and having no hope of support, no alternative remained but to capitulate. At about one o'clock, therefore, the fort was surrendered to the enemy and hostilities ceased. The troops marched out with the honours of war, and laid down their arms in the square. The officers being granted parole were quartered upon the inhabitants of the town, and the men were confined in the prisons of the city.

In these melancholy proceedings Lieut. Mitchell and Ensign Lucas were killed, and the regiment lost 91 men in killed and wounded.

In August, 1806, the second battalion embarked at 2nd bat.

1806. Glasgow for Ireland, and arrived at Belfast on the 1st of September.

1st bat. About the middle of September the Seventy-first were removed from Buenos Ayres into the interior. Brigadier-General Beresford, with his staff, and Lieut.-Colonel Pack, were placed at Luxon, from whence they subsequently effected their escape, upon learning that the removal of the prisoners still further up the country had been ordered.

1807. Lieut.-Colonel Pack was thus enabled to join the troops which had landed near Monte Video in January, 1807, under the command of Brigadier-General Sir Samuel Auchmuty, who at Lieut.-Colonel Pack's request, directed a board of naval and military officers to inquire into the particulars of his escape, by whom it was unanimously approved, and he was declared free to serve.

2nd bat. The second battalion was removed from Ireland to Scotland in January, 1807, but returned to Ireland in June following.

1st bat. In May, 1807, a further removal to the interior of the prisoners took place. The officers were collected at a college belonging to the Jesuits about forty leagues to the northward of Cordova, and entirely separated from their men. In this situation they remained until August following, when, just as they were ordered to prepare for a transfer to a station still more remote, the accounts of the convention entered into by Lieut.-General John Whitelocke were received, by which it was stipulated that the prisoners should be restored to liberty on condition that all the British forces should be withdrawn. It is scarcely necessary to remark that the prospect of being restored to liberty and friends was greatly damped by the military events which produced it, and which completely extinguished the ardent hopes of success that had been entertained from the arrival of the last British force in South America.

In September the whole of the officers and men were

reconducted to Buenos Ayres, from whence they were con- 1807.
veyed in boats to Monte Video, and there embarked in 1st bat.
transports with a view of returning to Europe.

It is a circumstance highly creditable to the character of the soldiers of the Seventy-first that, although so many powerful allurements were held out to induce them to remain in South America, but few individuals were found to swerve from their duty and allegiance to their King and country. The Spaniards were very fond of the Highlanders, particularly of those who were Catholics. One of these, named Donald Macdonald, overcome by solicitations, had almost agreed to remain at Buenos Ayres, but whilst wavering one of his companions sung to him "Lochaber no more;" the effect was irresistible; the tears started into poor Donald's eyes, and wiping them away, he exclaimed, "Na, na! I canna stay, I'd maybe return to Lochaber nae mair."

The fleet sailed immediately, and after a tedious and rough voyage of three months, the transports having the Seventy-first on board put into Cork Harbour in December, and on the 27th of that month the whole were landed, without uniform, clothing, arms, or accoutrements, and marched to Middleton under the command of Major Henry Tolley, Lieut.-Colonel Pack having previously returned to England from South America.

In March, 1808, the regiment proceeded from Middle- 1808.
ton to Cork, where its equipment in every respect was completed.

The second battalion embarked at Londonderry for 2nd bat.
Scotland on the 9th of April, 1808, after transferring 200 men to the first battalion, which raised the strength of the latter to nearly 900 rank and file.

On the 26th of April, whilst in garrison at Cork, new 1st bat.
colours, to replace those left in South America, were presented to the Seventy-first by Lieut.-General John Floyd,

1808. who had commanded the cavalry and advance in the campaign of 1790 in the East Indies.

The following animating and soldier-like address was made by the gallant General on the occasion:—

" Seventy-first!!

" I am directed to perform the honourable duty of presenting your colours.

" Brave Seventy-first, the world is well acquainted with
" your gallant conduct at the capture of Buenos Ayres in
" South America, under one of His Majesty's bravest
" Generals.

" It is well known that you defended your conquest
" with the utmost courage, good conduct, and discipline, to
" the last extremity. When diminished to a handful, hope-
" less of succour, and destitute of provisions, you were
" overwhelmed by multitudes, and reduced by the fortune
" of war to lose your liberty and your well-defended
" colours, but not your honour. Your honour, Seventy-first
" Regiment, remains unsullied.

" Your last act in the field covered you with glory.
" Your generous despair, calling upon your General to suffer
" you to die with arms in your hands, proceeded from the
" genuine spirit of British soldiers. Your behaviour in
" prosperity—your sufferings in captivity—and your faith-
" ful discharge of your duty to your King and country,
" are appreciated by all.

" You who now stand on this parade, in defiance of the
" allurements held out to base desertion, are endeared to
" the army and to the country, and your conduct will ensure
" you the esteem of all true soldiers—of all worthy men—
" and fill every one of you with honest martial pride.

" It has been my good fortune to have witnessed, in a
" remote part of the world, the early glories and gallant
" conduct of the Seventy-first Regiment in the field ; and

"it is with great satisfaction I meet you again with re- 1808.
" plenished ranks, with good arms in your hands, and with
" stout hearts in your bosoms.

" Look forward, officers and soldiers, to the achieve-
" ment of new honours and the acquirement of fresh fame!!

" Officers! be the friends and guardians of these brave
" fellows committed to your charge!!

" Soldiers! give your confidence to your officers. They
" have shared with you the chances of war; they have
" bravely bled along with you,—they will always do honour
" to themselves and you. Preserve your regiment's reputa-
" tion for valour in the field and regularity in quarters.

" I have now the honour to present the
    " Royal Colour.
    " This is the King's colour!!

" I have now the honour to present your regimental
" colour.

" This is the colour of the Seventy-first Regiment.

" May victory for ever crown these colours!!!"

The Peninsula was at this period the centre of political interest. Portugal, deserted by her government, and Spain betrayed, the people of each rose in arms to recover the national independence. Dissensions had arisen in the Royal family of Spain, occasioned by the sway of Emanuel Godoy, who bore the title of the "Prince of Peace." This Minister was dismissed, but the Court was unable to restore tranquillity. In this emergency the French Emperor was solicited to be umpire, and Napoleon ultimately placed the crown of Spain on his brother Joseph, who was transferred from the throne of Naples. The Spaniards flew to arms in consequence. The British Government resolved to aid the Spanish and Portuguese patriots, and a British army was ordered to proceed to the Peninsula, under the command of Lieut.-General Sir Arthur Wellesley. The first batta-

1808. lion of the Seventy-first Highlanders formed part of the force selected on this occasion.

It embarked at the Cove of Cork on the 17th of June, 1808, its strength consisting of 52 sergeants, 22 drummers, and 874 rank and file.

In June, 1808, His Majesty King George III was pleased to approve of the Seventy-first bearing the title of *Glasgow* in addition to the appellation of *Highland* regiment.*

In the first instance, the Seventy-first were brigaded with the Fifth, Thirty-eighth, and fifth battalion of the Sixtieth Regiment, under Brigadier-General Henry Fane, and sailed for Portugal, in conjunction with the forces destined to aid the Spaniards and Portuguese, on the 12th of July. After a favourable passage, the troops anchored in Mondego Bay in the beginning of August, and a landing was effected in the vicinity of the village of Frejus.

Early in the morning of the 4th of August a small picket of the enemy stationed in the neighbourhood fell back, and the operation of disembarking the troops was carried into effect without opposition. The army then moved on to a position across a deep sandy country, where it halted and encamped for the night.

At this period a change took place in the arrangement of the brigades, and the first battalion of the Seventy-first was placed, with the Thirty-sixth and Fortieth Regiments, in that commanded by Major-General Ronald Craufurd Ferguson.

The division under Major-General Sir Brent Spencer, K.B., from Cadiz, consisting of about 4,000 men, joined on the 8th of August; and, after a short halt, the army was again put in motion to occupy a more forward position, where it remained for some days. On the 17th

---

* The absurdly contradictory name of Glasgow Highland Light Infantry has not been in use for many years.

August the enemy, commanded by General Laborde, was encountered near Roleia. The position was attacked and carried with great loss to the French, who retreated to Torres Vedras.

1808.

The light company of the Seventy-first was the only part of the regiment engaged, the remainder being employed in manœuvring on the right flank of the French. It suffered a trifling loss, having but 1 man killed and 2 wounded.

The Seventy-first subsequently received the Royal authority to bear the word "Roleia" on the regimental colours and appointments, in commemoration of this victory.

Lieut.-General Sir Arthur Wellesley, after the battle of Roleia, did not pursue the enemy by the high roads, but, keeping to the right near the sea, marched to Vimiera to cover the landing of a brigade commanded by Major-General Anstruther, which was effected on the 20th of August.

The morning of the 21st of August was given up to the troops, in order to prepare and repose themselves. The men were engaged in washing and cleaning their equipments, when the approach of the enemy, moving to the left, was discovered at eight o'clock in the morning, and the brigades commanded by Major-General Ferguson, Brigadier-Generals Nightingall, Acland, and Bowes, were consequently moved across a valley from the heights on the west to those on the east of Vimiera.

Marshal Junot, Duke of Abrantes, moved on his army to the attack of the position, directing it on the British centre, where the Fiftieth Regiment was posted, and moving along the front gradually to the left until the whole line became engaged.

A short time previously to this, the soldiers of the brigade were ordered to sit down, with their arms in their hands, keeping their formation. The enemy in the meantime cannonaded the whole line, and pushed on his sharpshooters and infantry. To oppose the former, Major-General Ferguson ordered the left sections of the companies to move forward and skirmish. Upon the retreat of the enemy's sharpshooters, the action became general along the front of this brigade, and the whole moved forward to the attack. Nothing could surpass the steadiness of the troops on this occasion, and the general and commanding officers set a noble example, which was followed by all.

The grenadier company of the Seventy-first greatly distinguished itself, in conjunction with a subdivision of the light company of the Thirty-sixth Regiment. Captain Alexander Forbes, who commanded the grenadier company, was ordered to the support of some British artillery, and seizing a favourable opportunity, made a dash at a battery of the enemy's artillery immediately in his front. He succeeded in capturing five guns and a howitzer, with horses, caissons, and equipment complete. In this affair alone the grenadier company had Lieutenants John Pratt and Ralph Dudgeon and 13 rank and file wounded, together with 2 men killed.

The French made a daring effort to retake their artillery both with cavalry and infantry; but the gallant conduct of the grenadier company, and the advance of Major-General Ferguson's brigade, finally left the guns in the possession of those who had so gallantly captured them.

George Clark, one of the pipers of the regiment, and afterwards piper to the Highland Society of London, was severely wounded in this action, and being unable to accompany his corps in the advance against the enemy, he deliberately sat down, and unstrapping his pipes, called out, "Well my bra' lads, I can no farther wi' ye a fighting, but diel ha' my soul if ye sal want music," and immediately began playing "Up and war them a' Willie." He was afterwards presented with a handsome stand of pipes by the Highland Society. This is the second instance in which the pipèrs of the Seventy-first have behaved with particular gallantry, and evinced high feeling for the credit and honour of the corps.

1808.

During the advance of the battalion, several prisoners were taken, among whom was the French General Brennier, who surrendered himself on the columns giving way to corporal John McKay. The latter was afterwards promoted to an ensigncy in the Fourth West India Regiment.

The result of this battle was the total defeat of the enemy, who subsequently retreated on Lisbon, with the loss of twenty-one pieces of cannon, twenty-three ammunition waggons, with powder, shells, stores of all descriptions, and 20,000 rounds of musket ammunition, together with a great many officers and soldiers killed, wounded, and taken prisoners.

The conduct of the battalion, and of its commanding officer, Lieut.-Colonel Pack, was noticed in the public despatches, and the thanks of the Houses of Parliament were conferred on the troops.

The following officers of the Seventy-first were wounded in the battle of Vimiera : Captains Arthur Jones and Maxwell Mackenzie ; Lieutenants John Pratt, William Hartley, Augustus McIntyre, and Ralph Dudgeon ; Ensign James Campbell, and Acting Adjutant R. McAlpine. Twelve rank and file were killed ; six sergeants, and eighty-six rank and file wounded.

The Seventy-first subsequently received the royal authority to bear the word " Vimiera " on the regimental colour and appointments, in commemoration of this battle.

The *Convention of Cintra* was the result of this victory ; it was signed on the 30th of August, and by its provisions the French Army evacuated Portugal,

The British Army was ordered to move forward to Lisbon, some of the reinforcements for it having preceded it by water, and occupied the forts at the mouth of the

1808. Tagus. The French Army having by this convention fallen back on Lisbon, the British proceeded to the vicinity of Fort St. Julien, and encamped there.

All the objects of the expedition being carried into effect, and the French troops embarked for France, the British Army remained for some time at Lisbon and its vicinity. At this period (September) Lieut.-General Sir John Moore, having assumed the command, made dispositions for entering Spain.

The first battalion of the Seventy-first was now brigaded with the Thirty-sixth and Ninety-eighth Regiments, under Brigadier-General Catlin Craufurd, and placed in the division under the command of Lieut.-General the Honourable John Hope, afterwards the Earl of Hopetoun. On the 27th of October the division was put in motion, and after a short stay at Badajoz, resumed the march, proceeding by Merida, Truxillo, Jaraicejo, Puerto-de-Merivette, and crossing the Tagus at the bridge of Almaraz, directed its route upon Talavera-de-la-Reyna. From this town the column proceeded to the Escurial, seven leagues to the north-west of Madrid.

Intelligence was here received of the enemy's approach towards Madrid, and two companies of the Seventy-first, under Major Archibald Campbell, were pushed forward to occupy the important pass in the Guadarama Mountains, which separate Old from New Castile. After a halt of a few days, the division was put in motion over the Guadarama Pass to Villa Castin, at which place Lieut.-General the Honourable John Hope, in consequence of the intelligence which he received of the enemy's movements, made a night march to the left, by Avila and Peneranda, and finally proceeded to Alba-de-Tormes. At the latter place a junction was formed with a detachment from the army under Lieut.-General Sir John Moore, then at Salamanca. The army under Sir John Moore was shortly afterwards put in motion towards Valladolid, and subsequently to the 1808. left, to form a junction with Lieut.-General Sir David Baird's division, which had landed at Corunna.

Previously to this period, the Spanish Armies under General Blake, near Bilboa on the left, General Castanos in the centre, and General Palafox lower down the Ebro on the right, had been completely defeated. Lieut.-General Sir John Moore consequently made arrangements for a retreat on Portugal by Ciudad Rodrigo; but it having been represented to him that Madrid held out against the French, he was induced to effect a junction with Lieut.-General Sir David Baird, in order to make a diversion in favour of Madrid, by attacking Marshal Soult on the River Carion.

The British force, twenty-nine thousand strong, joined at Toro on the 21st of December, and on the 23rd of that month Sir John Moore advanced with the whole army. The cavalry had already met with that of the enemy, and the infantry was within two hours' march of him, when an intercepted letter informed the British Commander that Napoleon, who had entered Madrid on the 4th of December, was then in full march for Salamanca and Benevente. A retreat on Corunna, through Gallicia, was immediately decided on, that through Portugal being then impracticable.

Accordingly the several divisions marched towards the Esla, the greater part crossing by the bridge of Benevente. On the 26th of December, after a day's halt, the cavalry under Lieut.-General Lord Paget and Brigadier-General the Honourable Charles Stewart had an engagement with some of the Imperial Guards that had forded the River Esla under General Le Févre, who was made prisoner, with several of his men.

At this period the situation of the British Army was dispiriting in the extreme. In the midst of winter, in a dreary and desolate country, the soldiers chilled and

1808. drenched with the heavy rains, and wearied by long and rapid marches, were almost destitute of fuel to cook their victuals, and it was with extreme difficulty that they could procure shelter. Provisions were scarce, irregularly issued, and difficult of attainment. The waggons, in which were their magazines, baggage and stores, were often deserted in the night by the Spanish drivers, who were terrified by the approach of the French. Thus baggage, ammunition, stores, and even money were destroyed to prevent them falling into the hands of the enemy; and the weak, the sick, and the wounded were necessarily left behind. The Seventy-first suffered in proportion with the rest, and by weakness, sickness, and fatigue lost about 93 men.

1809. On the 5th of January, 1809, a position was taken up
1st bat. at Lugo, where some skirmishing occurred, in which three companies of the Seventy-first were engaged, and repulsed the enemy.

Lieut.-General Francis Dundas was appointed from the Ninety-fourth Regiment to be Colonel of the Seventy-first on the 7th of January, 1809, in succession to Lieut.-General Sir John Francis Cradock, K.B., removed to the Forty-third Regiment.

The retreat was again commenced on the 9th of January, and on the 11th the army, still nearly fifteen thousand strong, reached Corunna. The British Army, having accomplished one of the most celebrated retreats recorded in modern history, repulsing the pursuing enemy in all his attacks, and having traversed two hundred and fifty miles of mountainous country, accompanied by severe privation, was not destined to embark for England without a battle.

The transports not having arrived, a position was occupied in advance of Corunna, and some sharp skirmishing ensued, in which four companies of the Seventy-first were warmly engaged, and lost several men in killed and wounded. Lieutenant William Lockwood was severely 1809. wounded. On this ground the battle of Corunna was fought on the 16th of January; but the Seventy-first being placed on the extreme left of the British line, had little part in it. The result of the action was glorious to the British Army, but was darkened by the loss of Lieut.-General Sir John Moore, who received a severe wound during the battle, and died at ten o'clock on the same night. His remains were wrapped in a military cloak, and interred in the Citadel of Corunna, over which Marshal Soult, with the true feeling of a soldier, erected a monument.

Lieut.-General Sir David Baird, who succeeded to the command upon Sir John Moore being wounded, was also wounded, and the command devolved upon Lieut.-General the Honourable John Hope.

At eight o'clock on the night of the 16th of January the troops quitted their position, leaving the pickets posted and a few men to keep up-the fires, and then marched into Corunna, where they embarked for England on the following day.

In commemoration of this battle, and of the conduct of the battalion during the expedition, the Seventy-first, in common with the army employed under Lieut.-General Sir John Moore, received the royal authority to bear the the word "Corunna" on the regimental colour and appointments.

The thanks of both Houses of Parliament were conferred on the troops, and were communicated to Lieut.-Colonel Pack by Lieut.-General Sir David Baird in the following letter:—

"*Portsmouth, 30th January,* 1809.
" Sir,
"I have great pleasure in transmitting to you
" copies of letters from the Lord Chancellor and the
" Speaker of the House of Commons, enclosing the resolu-

1809. "tions of both Houses of Parliament, dated 25th of Janu-
"ary, 1809, which contain the thanks of those Houses to
"the army lately engaged before Corunna.

"In communicating to you, Sir, this most signal mark
"of the approbation of the Parliament of the United
"Kingdom of Great Britain and Ireland, allow me to
"add my warmest congratulations upon a distinction
"which you, and the corps under your command on
"that day, had a share in obtaining for His Majesty's
"service.

"I have, etc.,
(Signed) "DAVID BAIRD,
"*Lieut.-General.*

"*Officer commanding first battalion
"Seventy-first Highlanders.*"

After the battalion had landed at Ramsgate it was marched to Ashford, in Kent, where it continued for some time collecting the men, who, from contrary winds, were driven into different ports.

While at Ashford the battalion was brigaded with the Warwick Militia and the Ninety-first Regiment, under Brigadier-General the Baron de Rottenburg. Great sickness prevailed at this station, and Surgeon James Evans and several of the soldiers died of typhus fever.

On the 20th of March, 1809, the Royal authority was granted for the Seventy-first to be formed into a light infantry regiment, since which time it has been distinguished as the Highland Light Infantry.

The first battalion marched on the 27th of April, 1809, for Brabourne Lees Barracks, and was brigaded with the Sixty-eighth and Eighty-fifth Light Infantry Regiments. Every exertion was here made to increase the strength and improve the discipline of the corps. In June the first battalion was increased by a large reinforcement, consisting of several officers and 311 non-commissioned officers and privates from the second battalion, which continued to be stationed in North Britain. Several volunteers from the militia were also received at this period.

Immense preparations had been made by the British Government to fit out the most formidable armament that had for a long time proceeded from England. The troops, amounting to 40,000 men, were commanded by Lieut.-General the Earl of Chatham. The naval portion consisted of 39 ships of the line, 35 frigates, and numerous gunboats, bomb vessels, and other small craft, under Admiral Sir Richard Strachan. The object of the expedition was to obtain possession of the islands at the mouth of the Scheldt and to destroy the French ships in that river, with the docks and arsenals at Antwerp. The first battalion of the Seventy-first, towards the end of June, received orders to prepare for the above service, and marched on the 28th and 29th of that month in two divisions, encamping near Gosport.

On the 16th of July the battalion, consisting of 3 field officers, 6 captains, 27 subalterns, 5 staff, 48 sergeants, and 974 drummers and rank and file, embarked at Portsmouth on board His Majesty's ships *Belleisle* and *Impérieuse*, and towards the end of the month sailed for the Downs.

The battalion was brigaded, under Brigadier-General the Baron de Rottenburg, with the Sixty-eighth and Eighty-fifth Light Infantry, in the division commanded by Lieut.-General Alexander Mackenzie Fraser, and in the corps of Lieut.-General Sir Eyre Coote, K.B.

The expedition sailed from the Downs on the 28th of July, and having arrived off the Roompot Channel, preparations were made for landing; small craft to cover the landing were also sent in shore, and the light brigade, composed of the Sixty-eighth, Seventy-first, and Eighty-fifth Light Infantry, were landed under their fire. In an

1809. instant they were in contact with the enemy's sharpshooters, who fell back, skirmishing. Being pushed hard, four guns, with their equipment and several prisoners, were taken by two companies of the Seventy-first, under Captains George Sutherland and Henry Hall, and one company of the Eighty-fifth.

A battery and flag-staff on the coast were taken possession of by the tenth company of the Seventy-first, and in lieu of a flag a soldier's red jacket was hoisted on it.

This advance having succeeded at all points, and the enemy having fallen back on Flushing and Middleburg, the army was disembarked. The advance then dividing, proceeded by different routes. The Seventy-first moved by the sea dyke on a fort called Ter Veer, the situation and strength of which was not sufficiently known, an enemy's deserter having given but imperfect intelligence respecting it.

After nightfall the column continued to advance in perfect silence, with orders to attack the post with the bayonet, when, on a sudden the advance-guard fell in with an enemy's party, who came out for the purpose of firing some houses which overlooked the works. The column following the advance-guard had entered an avenue or road leading to the fort, when the advance commenced the action with the enemy, who, retiring within the place, opened a tremendous fire from his works with artillery and musketry. Some guns pointing down the road by which the battalion advanced did great execution, and the Seventy-first had Surgeon Charles Henry Quin killed, and about 18 men killed and wounded. The column, after some firing retired, and the place was the next day regularly invested by sea and land. It took three days to reduce, when it capitulated, with its stores and a garrison of 800 men.

Flushing having been invested on the 1st of August, the Seventy-first, after the surrender of Ter Veer, were ordered into the line of circumvallation, and placed on the extreme left, resting on the Scheldt. The preparations for the attack on the town having been completed, on the 13th a dreadful fire was opened from the batteries and bomb-vessels, and congreve-rockets having been thrown into the town, it was on fire in many places. The ships having joined in the attack, the enemy's fire slackened, and at length ceased. A summons being sent in, a delay was demanded, but, being rejected, the firing re-commenced.

On the 14th of August one of the outworks was carried at the point of the bayonet by a party of detachments and two companies of the Seventy-first under Lieut.-Colonel Pack.

In this affair, Ensign Donald Sinclair of the Seventy-first was killed; Captain George Spottiswoode and a few men were wounded.

Flushing, with its garrison of 6,000 men, capitulated on the 15th of August, and the right gate was occupied by a detachment of 300 men of the First or Royal Scots, and the left gate by a detachment of similar strength of the Seventy-first under Major Arthur Jones. The naval arsenal and some vessels of war which were on the stocks, fell into the hands of the British.

The Seventy-first proceeded shortly afterwards to Middleburg, where the battalion remained for a few days, when it was ordered to occupy Ter Veer, of which place Lieut.-Colonel Pack was appointed Commandant, and Lieutenant Henry Clements, of the Seventy-first, Town Major. The battalion remained doing duty in the garrison until this island, after destroying the works, etc., was finally evacuated on the 22nd of December.

On the 23rd of December the battalion embarked in transports and sailed for England, after a service of five months in a very unhealthy climate, which cost the battalion the loss of the following officers and men:—

1809.

	Officers.	Sergeants, Drummers, and Rank and File.
Died on service	1	57
Killed	2	19
Died after return home	2	9
	5	85

In passing Cadsand, that fort opened a fire on the transports, one of which, having part of the Seventy-first on board, was struck by a round shot which carried off Sergeant Steel's legs above the knees.*

On the 25th of December the first battalion of the Seventy-first disembarked at Deal, and marched to Brabourne-Lees barracks, in Kent, where it was again brigaded with the Sixty-eighth and Eighty-fifth Light Infantry, and was occupied in keeping itself in an efficient state for active service.

1810. Upon the Seventy-first being made light infantry, they were permitted to retain such parts of the national dress as might not be inconsistent with their duties as a light corps. A correspondence on the subject took place as follows between Lieut.-Colonel Pack and the Adjutant-General in April, 1810:—

"Sir,

" I beg leave to state that until I read the Adjutant-
" General's letter of the 31st January last, a copy of which
" I have the honour herewith to enclose, I did not think it
" possible any misconception could exist as to the Seventy-
" first being no longer considered a Highland Regiment,
" having myself clearly understood from His Royal High-
" ness the Duke of York and the present Commander-in-
" Chief that in becoming light infantry the corps was to be
" put, as to Colonel's allowances, clothing, and appoint-
" ments, exactly on the same establishment as English

* The correct number of rank and file wounded is not given.

"'regiments of the line, being only allowed to retain our
" name and such characteristics of the old corps as were in
" no way found objectionable, and out of which in point of
" 'esprit de corps' much good and no possible harm
" could arise, and it was under this impression that the
" bonnet cocked as a regimental cap was submitted to the
" Horse Guards for approval, and was sealed by the
" Adjutant-General for our use. With this security I
" should now rest satisfied, but on a point affecting the
" honour of the regiment, I cannot allow a shadow of
" doubt to rest. I have, therefore, to entreat the Com-
" mander-in-Chief that unquestionable authority may be
" given for our wearing the bonnet so cocked, for retaining
" our pipes, and still dressing our pipers in the Highland
" garb. It cannot be forgotten how those pipes were ob-
" tained, and how constantly the regiment has upheld its
" title to them. These are the honourable characteristics
" alluded to, which must preserve to future times the pre-
" cious remains of the old corps, and of which I feel con-
" fident His Majesty never will have reason to deprive the
" Seventy-first Regiment.

    " I have the honour to be,
      " Sir,
    "Your most obedient servant,
      (Signed)   "D. PACK,
       " *Lieut.-Colonel Seventy-first*
         " *Regiment.*"

" *The Adjutant-General of the Forces,*
 " *Horse Guards London.*"

1810.

      " *Horse Guards,*
" Sir,   " 12*th April*, 1810.
  " Having submitted to the Commander-in-Chief
" your letter of the 4th instant, I am directed to state that

1810. "there is no objection to the Seventy-first being denominated "Highland Light Infantry Regiment, or to their retaining "their pipes, and the Highland garb for the pipers, and "that they will, of course, be permitted to wear caps "according to the pattern which was lately approved and "sealed by authority.

"I have, &c.,
(Signed) "WILLIAM WYNWARD,
"*Deputy Adjutant-General.*
"*Lieut.-Colonel Pack, Seventy-first
Regiment.*"

On the 8th of May, 1810, the first battalion marched to Deal Barracks, where every exertion was continued to render it fit for active service. Here the battalion was deprived of the services of Lieut.-Colonel Pack, who was appointed a brigadier in the Portuguese army under Marshal William Carr Beresford, afterwards General the Viscount Beresford.

Nothing of moment occurred until the early part of September, when the battalion received orders to hold six companies in readiness for foreign service. They were prepared accordingly by drafting into them, from the companies which were to remain at home, the most effective officers and men, several not having recovered from the Walcheren fever.

The following were the companies selected and completed for foreign service, namely:—

1st or Capt.	McIntyre's.	4th or Capt.		Walker's.
2nd "	Hall's.	6th	"	Spottiswoode's.
3rd "	Adamson's	10th	"	Lewis Grant's.

They consisted of 2 field officers, 6 captains, 15 lieutenants, 7 ensigns, 4 staff, 38 sergeants, 12 drummers, and 603 rank and file.

On the 14th of September the above companies embarked in the Downs on board the Melpomene and St. Fiorenzo frigates, three companies with the staff, and Brevet Lieut.-Colonel Nathaniel Levett Peacocke, on board the former; the remaining three companies, under Brevet Lieut.-Colonel Thomas Reynell, afterwards colonel of the regiment, on board the latter. They sailed on the following day for Lisbon, and entered the Tagus on the 25th of September, after a short and pleasant passage. The companies were disembarked on the following day, and quartered in the San Benito and Espirito Santo convents.

The greatest exertions were made to complete the companies in field equipment, bât-mules, &c., which being effected, the detachment marched from Lisbon on the 2nd of October to Mafra, where it was shortly afterwards joined by Lieut.-Colonel the Honourable Henry Cadogan, who assumed the command, and Lieut.-Colonel Peacocke returned to the second battalion in North Britain. The detachment being ordered to join the army under Lieut.-General Viscount Wellington, then retreating before Marshal Massena, Prince of Essling, marched from Mafra on the 8th of October, and on the 10th of that month effected the junction at Sobral, where it was brigaded with the Fiftieth and Ninety-second Regiments under Major-General Sir William Erskine, in the first division under Lieut.-General Sir Brent Spencer, K.B.

The army having retired into a position in the rear of Sobral, that place was occupied by the Seventy-first, having for its support the Fiftieth and Ninety-second Regiments and Major-General Alan Cameron's brigade. On the 12th of October the pickets were violently attacked by the enemy's advance, and retired skirmishing. In the meantime the place was ordered to be evacuated, and the pickets having joined, the Seventy-first took up a position on the outside, within musket-shot of the town. In this affair the detachment had 8 men killed and 34 wounded.

1810. In this position the Seventy-first continued, when on the 14th of October they were again attacked with the greatest impetuosity, and charged with the bayonet. The enemy was completely repulsed, with very considerable loss in killed and wounded, being chased to the spot from which he made the attack. Both parties resumed their original position.

In Viscount Wellington's despatch reporting this affair, the names of Lieut.-Colonel the Honourable Henry Cadogan, commanding the Seventy-first, and that of Brevet Lieut.-Col. Thomas Reynell, were particularly mentioned.

A soldier of the sixth company, named John Rea, behaved on this occasion in the most gallant manner, and particularly distinguished himself, for which he received a silver medal with the following inscription:—" To John " Rea, for his exemplary courage and good conduct as a " soldier at Sobral, 14th October, 1810."

On the 15th of October the Seventy-first was ordered to withdraw into the position at Zibriera, which was in continuation of the lines of Torres Vedras. In this celebrated position, which bid defiance to the French army, the troops were constantly on the alert, occupied in rendering it as strong as circumstances would admit, and in observing the motions of the enemy.

Marshal Massena did not think proper to attack the British army in this stronghold, and occupied his time in reconnaissances and demonstrations, until compelled, through want of provisions and consequent sickness of his troops, to abandon his designs, and retire to a position in his rear. This object he finally effected in a masterly manner, in the night, between the 14th and 15th of November, followed by the allied forces. Both armies thus evacuated positions on which the attention of Europe had been fixed, and which they had occupied for a month in presence of each other.

The division in which the six companies of the 1810. Seventy-first were placed advanced by the route of Alemquer, Cartajo, Atataya, and Almoster, and halted in and about the latter place from the 20th to the 26th of November, inclusive. The enemy, in the mean time, retired to an extremely strong position at and in the vicinity of Santarem, where Marshal Massena halted, although threatened by Viscount Wellington, who, after some manœuvring, took up a position immediately in the enemy's front, having his head-quarters at Cartajo, and the different corps of the army in the villages. The brigade to which the Seventy-first belonged occupied Alquintrinha.

At this place the Seventy-first remained in quarters 1811. until March, 1811, at which period the army, having been 1st bat. reinforced, was about to resume the offensive, when the enemy retired during the night of the 5th of March, taking the same road, through Estremadura, by which he entered Portugal.

The British army accordingly marched in pursuit of Marshal Massena, and the brigade in which was the Seventy-first accompanied it, moving by Redinha, Miranda de Corvo, and Saryedes, passing the Coa, a little above Sabugal, upon the 5th of April, and on the 9th arrived at Albergaria, a small town on the frontiers of Spain. The Seventy-first remained in Albergaria until the 2nd of May, when the enemy, having been strongly reinforced, moved off from Salamanca, and on that day crossed the frontier with a large convoy of provisions for Almeida, then closely invested by the Portuguese forces under Brigadier-General Pack.

In consequence of this movement the allied army broke up its cantonments on the Azava, and formed in order of battle upon the high ground behind the Duas Casas, the left extending to the high road to Almeida, which crossed the river by a ford near Fort Concepcion, and the right

1811. keeping up a communication with the bridge at Sabugal; opposite the centre the village of Fuentes d'Onor was strongly occupied by light infantry.

Upon the 3rd of May the French took post on the opposite side of the valley of the Duas Casas, their left fronting Fuentes d'Onor, and their right extending about two miles and a half to Almeida. In the afternoon of the 3rd of May they attacked Fuentes d'Onor with much vigour. That post was defended with the greatest bravery, until the light companies, being worn out and harassed by repeated attacks, were obliged to retire, and the enemy possessed himself of the lower part of the village.

The Seventy-first was now ordered up in support, and, commanded by Lieut.-Colonel the Honourable Henry Cadogan, charged the enemy through the village and across the Duas Casas, taking ten officers and about a hundred men prisoners. The corps retained its conquest that night and the whole of the next day, but upon Sunday, the 5th of May, the French having succeeded in turning some troops to the immediate right, was obliged to give way; but having been promptly supported by the Seventy-fourth and Eighty-eighth Regiments, it again advanced, took possession of and retained the village until the conclusion of the action.

A struggle of such duration could not be carried on without great loss, and the Seventy-first suffered severely. It went into action about 320 strong, and lost nearly one-half of its number in killed and wounded.

The Seventy-first had Lieutenants John Consell, William Houston, and John Graham, and Ensign Donald John Kearns, together with 4 sergeants and 22 rank and file killed. Captains Peter Adamson and James McIntyre, Lieutenants William McCraw, Humphrey Fox, and Robert Law (Adjutant), Ensigns Charles Cox, John Vandeleur, and Carique Lewin, 6 sergeants, 3 buglers, and 100 rank and file, were wounded. 2 officers, with several men, were taken prisoners. 1811.

In commemoration of the gallantry displayed in this prolonged action, the Seventy-first subsequently received the royal authority to bear the words " Fuentes d'Onor " on the regimental colour and appointments.

The following letter from Lord Fitzroy Somerset will serve to show the opinion entertained by Lord Wellington of the conduct of the Seventy-first on this occasion.

"*Villa Formosa, 8th May,* 1811.
" Sir,
" Lord Wellington being highly gratified with the con-
" duct of the Seventy-first Regiment, has directed me to
" request that you will transmit to me the name of a non-
" commissioned officer who may be eligible for a commis-
" sion, in order that his Lordship may recommend him for
" an Ensigncy on the present occasion.
" I have the honour to be, Sir,
" Your most obedient servant,
" FITZROY SOMERSET.
" *Lieut.-Colonel*
" *The Honourable Henry Cadogan,*
" *Seventy-first Regiment."*

According to his Lordship's recommendation, Quarter-master-Sergeant William Gavin was shortly afterwards promoted to an ensigncy in the regiment.

The Seventy-first upon the 14th returned to their old quarters at Albergaria, and remained there until the 26th of May, when the brigade was ordered to the Alemtejo frontier, as a reinforcement to Marshal Sir William Beresford's army, at this time besieging Badajoz, and threatened by the advance of Marshal Soult from the south of Spain.

On the 15th of May, 1811, the second battalion 2nd bat.

F

1811. embarked at Leith for South Britain, arrived at Ramsgate on the 23rd of that month, and remained stationed in England for nearly two years.

1st bat. The first battalion, upon its route southward, crossed the Tagus on the 31st of May, and arrived near Albuhera on the 14th June, having passed through Portalegre, Aronches, Campo Mayor, and Talavera Real.

The sanguinary battle of Albuhera, fought on the 16th of May, had obliged Marshal Soult to retire previously to the arrival of the reinforcements, which being considered no longer necessary, the battalion retired to Elvas, where it remained two days, moving to Toro de Moro on the 19th of June, where it remained for a month. At this encampment a detachment of 350 men, with a proportion of officers, joined from the second battalion then stationed at Deal.

About this period the first battalion became a part of the army, under Lieut.-General Rowland (afterwards Viscount) Hill. The junction of the armies of Marshals Marmont and Soult having obliged Viscount Wellington to raise the siege of Badajoz, which had been resumed after the battle of Albuhera, the battalion, in co-operation with his Lordship's retrograde movement, retired to Borba on 20th of July. Here it remained until the 1st of September, when it moved to Portalegre, and thence marched to Castello de Vido, on the 4th of October.

A detachment from Marshal Soult's army, under General Girard, having been levying contributions in Spanish Estremadura, Lieut.-General Rowland Hill, with a view of putting a stop to his movements, broke up his cantonment at Portalegre, upon the 22nd of October, proceeding by Albuquerque and Malpartida. On the 27th, when, within a moderate march of the enemy at Arroyo-dos-Molinos, he halted his troops, and, at night, breaking up his bivouac, made a flank movement close to the road by which the French intended to march on the following morning. In that position he awaited the approach of day, when on the 28th of October, the British marched directly on the rear of the town with such celerity that the cavalry pickets were attacked before they had time to mount. 1811.

The French main body, though in the act of filing out, had so little intimation of danger, that the officers and men were surrounded before their formation was effected, and to seek safety they individually dispersed. Many of them were killed, and about 1,400 were taken prisoners. All the enemy's artillery and baggage were captured. General Brun, and Colonel the Prince of Aremberg, together with several other officers, were among the prisoners.

In this brilliant affair the Seventy-first was one of the three corps that advanced through the centre of the town, and were, therefore, principally engaged; but the enemy, from his complete surprise, being unable to make a combined resistance, the British sustained but a trifling loss.

The battalion subsequently returned to Portalegre, where it arrived early in November. Although the Thirty-fourth Regiment was allowed to inscribe the words, "Arroyo dos Molinos" on its colours, still, for some inexplicable reason, the same privilege has always been refused to the other regiments that were present at that action.

Lieut.-General Hill, on the 7th of November, issued the following General Order:—

"*Portalegre, 7th November*, 1811.

" Lieut.-General Hill has great satisfaction in congra-
" tulating the troops on the success which has attended
" their recent operations in Estremadura, and in so doing
" he cannot but endeavour to do justice to the merits of
" those through whose exertions it has been obtained. A
" patient, willing endurance of forced and night marches,
" during the worst of weather, and over bad roads, of
" bivouacs in wet weather, oftentimes without cover and

1811. "without fire, and a strict observance of discipline, are
"qualities, however, common in British soldiers, which the
"Lieut.-General cannot pass unnoticed. Having on this
"occasion witnessed the exertion of them in no ordinary
"degree, he feels that nothing but the most zealous atten-
"tion of commanding officers, the goodwill and zealous
"spirit of the non-commissioned officers and soldiers, could
"produce such an effect, and he requests they will, generally
"and individually, accept his warmest thanks, particularly
"those corps which were engaged in the action of Arroyo
"dos Molinos, whose silent attention to orders, when pre-
"paring to attack, and when manœuvring before the
"enemy, could not but excite his notice, and give them an
"additional claim on him."

Letters from the Secretary of State, dated the 2nd, and from His Royal Highness the Duke of York, Commander-in-Chief, dated the 6th December, were promulgated, expressive of His Royal Highness the Prince Regent's approbation and thanks to Lieut.-General Hill, and the troops under his command, for their brilliant operations on the recent expedition in Spanish Estremadura, in having totally surprised and defeated the enemy, under General Girard.

Viscount Wellington, having made preparations for the recapture of Ciudad Rodrigo, concentrated the main body of the army in that neighbourhood, and the troops, under Lieut.-General Hill, were therefore ordered to divert the enemy's attention in the south.

The first battalion of the Seventy-first remained at Portalegre, until the 25th of December, when the brigade moved into Estremadura, for the purpose of expelling the French, who were ravaging the country. After the performance of this duty, the battalion returned to its former quarters at Portalegre, in February, 1812.

Upon the 19th of March, 1812, the battalion moved northward to Castello Branco, where it remained for about a week, and afterwards returned for the last time to Portalegre. The Earl of Wellington having made arrangements for the third siege of Badajoz, Lieut.-General Sir Rowland Hill's corps was destined to cover his movements, and with that view proceeded on the 21st of March towards Merida, and afterwards to Don Benito, where the troops remained for a few days; but upon the approach of Marshal Soult with a large army, with the intention of raising the siege, Lieutenant-General Hill retired upon Albuhera, through Arroyo de San Servan and Talavera Real.

1812. 1st bat.

Badajoz having been assaulted and carried by the troops, under the Earl of Wellington, on the night of the 6th of April, after a sanguinary conflict, the movement of Marshal Soult was rendered nugatory, and the troops under his orders retired into Andalusia.

Marshal Marmont, having, during the progress of the siege, penetrated into the province of Beira, and threatened Ciudad Rodrigo and Almeida, the Earl of Wellington, after the fall of Badajoz, crossed the Tagus, leaving Sir Rowland Hill's force to watch Marshal Soult, which took post at Almendralejos for that purpose.

The battalion was stationed at this town, from the 13th of April until the 11th of May. It having then become expedient to render the communications between the French armies on the north and south of the Tagus as precarious as possible, by the destruction of the bridge of boats at Almaraz, the corps under Lieut.-General Sir Rowland Hill, being the most disposable and convenient force, was accordingly ordered on this important service.

The French, feeling the importance of this bridge to their mutual strength and security, had surrounded it on both sides of the river with formidable enclosed works, having in the interior of them casemated and loop-holed

1812. towers. The troops appointed for these strong works, consequently, anticipated an arduous struggle.

Upon the 12th of May the corps broke up from Almendralejos, and marching by Truscillo and Jaraicejo, reached on the 18th of that month the Sierra, 5 miles from Almaraz, on which stands the Castle of Mirabete. This post was so strongly fortified that it blocked up the only road to Almaraz for the passage of artillery, which was considered by the enemy absolutely necessary for the destruction of the works. Sir Rowland Hill thought otherwise, and ascertaining that infantry could cross the Sierra by a track through Roman Gordo, he left his artillery, and descended at night with a column of 2,000 men. The leading company arrived at dawn of day, close to the principal fort, built on a height a few hundred yards in front of the *tête de pont*, but such were the difficulties of the road, that a considerable time elapsed before the rear closed, during which the troops were fortunately sheltered by a ravine, unseen by the enemy.

On the 19th May the Fiftieth Regiment, and the left wing of the Seventy-first, having been provided with ladders, were appointed to escalade the works of Fort Napoleon, supported by the right wing of the Seventy-first and the Ninety-second Regiment.

From a feint made upon Mirabete, the French were aware that an enemy was in the neighbourhood. The garrison on the alert immediately opened a heavy fire, and vigorously resisted the efforts made to push up the escarp; but the moment the first men gained a footing on the parapet, the enemy took to flight. The whole of this brilliant affair was completed in the short space of 15 minutes, and with little loss. The Seventy-first had Captain Lewis Grant, with 1 sergeant and 7 rank and file killed; Lieutenants William Lockwood and Donald Ross, 3 sergeants, and 29 rank and file were wounded.

The names of 36 non-commissioned officers and soldiers 1812. of the Seventy-first were inserted in regimental orders for conspicuous bravery upon this occasion, and the Royal authority was subsequently granted for the word "Almaraz," to be borne on the regimental colour and appointments.

The following orders were issued upon this occasion :—

"*Bivouac, near Fort Napoleon,*
"*19th May,* 1812.

" BRIGADE ORDER.

" Major-General Howard cannot delay expressing his
" warmest acknowledgments to Lieut.-Colonel Stewart and
" Major Harrison, of the Fiftieth Regiment, and Major
" Cother, of the Seventy-first Regiment, who commanded
" the three columns of attack this morning on Fort Napo-
" leon, and the works on the Tagus, for the gallant and dis-
" tinguished manner in which they led the columns intrusted
" to them, as well as to all the other officers, non-commis-
" sioned officers, and privates, for their bravery and good
" conduct, which produced the brilliant result of the cap-
" ture of the works in question."

"*Truxillo, May 22nd,* 1812.

" GENERAL ORDER.

" Lieut.-General Sir Rowland Hill congratulates the
" troops on the success which has attended their exertions
" in the present expedition. Every object for which it was
" undertaken has been attained, and in the manner most
" desirable and effectual. It is highly gratifying to the
" Lieut.-General to report on this occasion his admiration
" of the discipline and the valour of the troops under his
" command. The chance of war gave to the Fiftieth and
" Seventy-first Regiments the most conspicuous share in
" these events, who nobly profited by the opportunity;
" but the Lieut.-General is satisfied that the same zeal and

1812. "the same spirit would have been found in every corps if
"there had been occasion for bringing them into play.

"The Lieut.-General has not failed to report to his
"Excellency the Commander of the Forces the particulars
"of this brilliant service, and the good conduct of all those
"concerned in it. He will, therefore, not say more at
"present than to express his warmest thanks for the
"assistance which he has received from all ranks; and he
"is confident, when it shall again be his good fortune to
"lead them against the enemy, he shall have to report
"conduct equally honourable to them and equally advan-
"tageous to their country."

The following is an extract from Lieut.-General Sir
Rowland Hill's despatch to Lord Wellington:—
"I cannot sufficiently praise the conduct of the Fiftieth
"and Seventy-first Regiments to whom the assaults fell,
"the constant steady manner in which they formed and
"advanced and carried the place was worthy of those
"distinguished corps and the officers who led them."

The bridge and works in the neighbourhood of Almaraz
having been completely destroyed, the Seventy-first returned to Truxillo, where they remained a few days, then
moved to Merida, and afterwards to Almendralejos. Lieut.-
General Sir Rowland Hill's force having received orders to
make a diversion in the south, while the main army was
moving northward on Salamanca, the battalion again
moved from Almendralejos to the borders of Andalusia,
through Llerena. On this march, the advanced parties of
cavalry were constantly skirmishing with the enemy, but
the Seventy-first was not engaged.

From Llerena the battalion returned to Zafra, whence,
after a short halt, it proceeded to Villa Franca, and finally
to Don Benito. In these marches through Estremadura,
the weather was oppressively hot, and, joined to the clouds

of dust raised by the troops, was so fatiguing that it was considered expedient at one time to move by night, and thus these inconveniences were alleviated.

While the force under Lieut.-General Sir Rowland Hill had been thus employed, the allied army, under the Earl of Wellington, had gained a victory on the 22nd of July over the French at Salamanca, for which he was advanced to the dignity of Marquis.

From Don Benito, the battalion moved upon the 13th of September, and passing through Truxillo, Talavera, and Toledo, arrived at Aranjuez upon the 1st of October, from which place, after a halt of three weeks, it moved to Ponte Duenna, further up the Tagus.

The sudden approach of the united armies of Marshals Soult and Suchet rendered a speedy retreat necessary, and the division accordingly retired from Ponte Duenna in the night of the 28th of October, moving to form a junction with the army of the Marquis of Wellington, who had now relinquished the siege of Burgos. Near Madrid, the division halted for a short period, when, being joined by the garrison of that city, the troops retired leisurely by the Guadarama Pass on Alba de Tormes. This town, the Seventy-first occupied from the 7th to the 13th of November, and during that period sustained a loss in action with the enemy of 1 sergeant and 6 rank and file killed; 1 bugler and 5 rank and file wounded.

The army having received orders to retire on Portugal, the battalion abandoned this post, arriving at Coria upon the 1st of December, where the retreat terminated. In this quarter, the Seventy-first continued until the 13th of December, at which time they were pushed forward to Puerto de Bannos, where they were joined by a draft of 150 men from the second battalion.

While stationed at this post, an attempt was made, in February, 1813, by the French, to surprise Bejar, then

1813. occupied by the Fiftieth regiment. The Seventy-first were ordered forward to support, but previously to their arrival that brave regiment had driven back the enemy and completely foiled his efforts.

2nd bat. On the 18th of March, 1813, the second battalion of the Seventy-first embarked at Gravesend for North Britain, and arrived at Leith on the 23rd of that month.

1st bat. Upon the 5th of April, the Seventy-first changed quarters with the Fiftieth regiment, and continued to occupy Bejar until the 21st of May, at which period the army broke up from its winter quarters for active operations. The battalion on its advance moved by Salamanca and Toro, and encamped at La Puebla on the 20th of June, the evening before the memorable battle of Vittoria.

Upon the morning of the 21st of June, the two armies being in position, the Seventy-first was ordered to ascend the heights of La Puebla, to support the Spanish forces under General Morillo. They accordingly advanced in open column, and having formed line, were immediately hotly engaged with the enemy, and upon this occasion suffered an irreparable loss in the fall of their Commanding Officer the Honourable Colonel Henry Cadogan, who fell mortally wounded while leading his men to the charge, and being unable to accompany the battalion, requested to be carried to a neighbouring eminence, from which he might take a last farewell of them and the field. In his dying moments, he earnestly inquired if the French were beaten, and on being told by an officer of the regiment who stood by supporting him, that they had given way at all points, he ejaculated, " God bless my brave countrymen," and immediately expired.

While recording the deep sense of sorrow which the Seventy-first experienced in the loss of a commanding officer who had so often fought at their head, and whose devoted gallantry had so frequently called forth their admiration, it is but a meet tribute to the memory of that brave officer to extract from the despatch of the Marquis of Wellington the following expressions of his Lordship's regret at his loss :

1813.

"And I am concerned to report that the Honourable "Lieut.-Colonel Cadogan has died of a wound which he "received. In him His Majesty has lost an officer of great "zeal and tried gallantry, who had already acquired the "respect and regard of the whole profession, and of whom "it might be expected that if he had lived he would have "rendered the most important services to his country."

After the fall of the Lieut.-Colonel, the Seventy-first continued advancing, and driving the enemy from the heights, until the force which was opposed to them became so unequal, and the loss of the battalion so severe, that it was obliged to retire upon the remainder of the brigade. In the performance of this arduous duty, the battalion suffered very severely, having had 1 field officer, 1 captain, 2 lieutenants, 6 sergeants, 1 bugler, and 78 rank and file killed; 1 field officer, 3 captains, 7 lieutenants, 13 sergeants, 2 buglers, and 255 rank and file were wounded.

The officers killed were Colonel the Honourable Henry Cadogan, Captain Henry Hall, Lieutenants Humphrey Fox and Colin Mackenzie. Those wounded were Brevet Lieut.-Colonel Charles Cother, Captains Samuel Reed, Joseph Thomas Pidgeon, William Alexander Grant, Lieutenants Alexander Duff, Loftus Richards, John McIntyre, Charles Cox, William Torriano, Norman Campbell, and Thomas Commeline.

Lieut.-General Sir William Stuart, on subsequently receiving the thanks of the House of Commons for his gallantry at Vittoria, thus recorded the bravery of this regiment on that day, in the course of his answer to the Speaker :—

1813. "I cannot advert to that battle and not submit to the "memory, and, if I may use the term, to the affection of "this House the name of one gallant officer upon whom "the brunt of this contest particularly fell—I mean, Sir, "the late Colonel Cadogan; the fall of that officer was "glorious, as his last moments were marked by the success "of a favourite regiment upon the magnanimity of whose "conduct he kept his eyes fixed during the expiring hour "of a well-finished life."

On this occasion the French suffered a great loss of men, together with all their artillery, baggage, and stores. King Joseph, whose carriage and court equipage were seized, had barely time to escape on horseback. The defeat was the most complete that the French had sustained in the Peninsula. It was this victory which gained a bâton for the Marquis of Wellington, who was appointed a Field-Marshal. In a most flattering letter, the Prince Regent, in the name and behalf of His Majesty, thus conferred the honour:—

"You have sent me among the trophies of your un-"rivalled fame the staff of a French Marshal, and I send "you in return that of England." This was in allusion to the bâton of Marshal Jourdon, which was taken by the Eighty-seventh Regiment at Vittoria.

The Seventy-first subsequently received the Royal authority to bear the word "Vittoria" on the regimental colour and appointments, in commemoration of this signal victory.

When the Seventy-first paraded on the morning of the 22nd of June, the dreadful havoc made by the action of the preceding day became painfully manifest, and an universal gloom was thrown over all, at missing from their ranks nearly 400 brave comrades who had been either killed or wounded on the heights of La Puebla.

The enemy having been completely beaten at all points

was forced to retreat in confusion on Pampeluna, and the British army immediately followed in pursuit. The battalion in this advance arrived at Pampeluna on the 29th of June, and shortly afterwards followed, as part of Sir Rowland Hill's army, a large force of the enemy, who were retreating into France by the valley of Bastan. During this forward movement the Seventy-first had some skirmishing in the valley of Elizondo, but without loss. Upon the 8th of July the Seventy-first arrived at the heights of Maya, from whence, for the first time, they had the cheering prospect of beholding the empire of France extended under them in all its fertile beauty. Joy was diffused through every heart: every trial and danger was forgotten while viewing this splendid and gratifying sight. Upon these heights the battalion was encamped until the 25th of July.

1813.

Marshal Soult having been selected by Napoleon for the command of the French army in Spain, with the rank of "Lieutenant of the Emperor," that officer used the most active exertions for its re-organization, and made immediate arrangements for forcing the British position in the Pyrenees. With this view he advanced in person with a large force against the right, stationed at Roncesvalles, and detached Count D'Erlon with about 13,000 men to attack the position of Maya.

The Count D'Erlon, upon the 25th of July, advanced against the right of the Maya heights, where the ridges of the mountains branched off towards his camp. The force at this point was not sufficient to resist such formidable numbers, and the reserve being posted at some distance to watch passes of importance, which could not be left wholly unguarded, was brought up by battalions as the pressure increased.

The intrepidity with which these attacks were met, and the obstinate bravery with which every inch of ground was

1813. disputed, were obliged at last to yield to overwhelming numbers; but although the troops were forced to retrograde, yet in their retreat they took advantage of every rising ground, and disputed it with the utmost tenacity. At the commencement of this attack a part of the first battalion of the Seventy-first Regiment was detached to a neighbouring high peak, under the command of Major William Fitzgerald of the Eighty-second Regiment, and was strengthened by a company of that corps. Lieut.-General the Honourable Sir William Stewart, in his report to Lieut.-General Sir Rowland Hill, thus expressed himself respecting these men:—" I cannot too warmly praise the "conduct of that field officer (Major Fitzgerald) and that "of his brave detachment. They maintained the position "to the last, and were compelled, from the want of ammu-"nition, to impede the enemy's occupation of the rock by "hurling stones at them."

In another part of this communication, the Lieut.-General thus alluded to the Eighty-second Regiment and to the first brigade, which was composed of the Fiftieth, Seventy-first, and Ninety-second Regiments:—

" I feel it my duty to recommend to your attention, and "favourable report to the Commander of the Forces, the "conduct and spirit of Colonel Grant, and of his brave "corps, the Eighty-second Regiment; also the whole of "the first brigade, than which His Majesty's army possesses "not men of more proved discipline and courage. The "wounds of him, and every commanding officer in that "brigade, were attended with circumstances of peculiar "honour to each of them, and to those under their "orders."

The following is a list of the killed and wounded in the action of the 25th of July, as nearly as could be ascertained:—

3 sergeants and 54 rank and file killed; 6 sergeants, 1 bugler, and 76 rank and file wounded.

The Seventy-first continued retiring until the 30th, when Lieut.-General Sir Rowland Hill took up a strong position beyond Lizasso. In this post he was attacked with much spirit by the enemy, who at the same time, by manœuvring on the left flank, rendered necessary a change of position to a range of heights near Eguaros, which all the efforts of the French failed to carry. Upon this occasion the Seventy-first was seriously engaged, and had 1 sergeant and 23 rank and file killed; 2 sergeants, 1 bugler, and 33 rank and file were wounded.

The enemy having been foiled in all the objects of his attack found it necessary, in his turn, to retreat, moving on the 31st of July by the pass of Doña Maria, where he left a strong corps in an excellent position. This force was immediately attacked by the columns of Lieut.-Generals Sir Rowland Hill and the Earl of Dalhousie, and dislodged after a gallant resistance. In the action of this day the first brigade, consisting of the Fiftieth, Seventy-first, and Ninety-second Regiments, had the honour of bearing its share and of distinguishing itself. The Seventy-first had 1 sergeant and 29 rank and file killed; 2 sergeants and 45 rank and file were wounded.

The battalion now returned to the heights of Maya, from whence, after a halt of a few days, it moved to Roncesvalles.

Previously to this change of quarters, an order was issued by Lieut.-General Sir Rowland Hill, relative to the conduct of the troops in the actions of the Pyrenees, of which the following is a copy:—

"*Arrizi, August 3rd*, 1813.
" GENERAL ORDER.

" Lieut.-General Sir Rowland Hill requests that the
" officers, non-commissioned officers, and privates of the

1813. "corps of the army under his command will accept his "best thanks for the gallant conduct they have displayed "during the late active and interesting operations.

"The chance of service has placed the troops under his "command in situations where they were exposed to an "immense superiority of forces, a circumstance unavoidable "in operations so extensive as those in which this army "has been engaged; and it has at all times been necessary "to cede ground to the enemy. The Lieut.-General, how- "ever, has the satisfaction of knowing that the troops have "on every occasion maintained their high character; that "they have only withdrawn from their positions by superior "orders, and then it has been invariably attended with "circumstances highly creditable to them. The Lieut.- "General has not failed to report to the Commander of the "Forces the details of the several affairs in which the corps "have been engaged, and he knows that their services are "duly appreciated by his Excellency."

The Royal authority was subsequently granted to the Seventy-first to bear the word "Pyrenees" on the regimental colour and appointments, in commemoration of the services of the first battalion in the actions of the 25th, 30th, and 31st of July, which have been designated the "*Battles of the Pyrenees.*"

In these actions the Seventy-first had Lieutenant Alexander Duff killed, Major Maxwell Mackenzie, Captains Leslie Walker and Alexander Grant, Lieutenants Thomas Park, John Roberts, William Woolcombe, William Peacocke, and Anthony Pack, wounded.

The following "Morning Reports" of the 14th of June and 7th of August, the former being prior to the battle of Vittoria, and the latter a few days subsequent to the actions in the Pyrenees, will show how the ranks of the Seventy-first were thinned within a period of less than two months:—

	Sergeants.	Buglers.	Rank and File.
14th June, 1813, present and fit for duty	54	21	909
7th August, 1813, ditto	21	15	356
Decrease	33	6	553

For nearly three months the battalion was encamped on the heights of Roncesvalles, during which period St. Sebastian and Pampeluna were captured. The men were principally employed during this interval in the construction of block houses and batteries, and the formation of roads for the artillery.

In the early part of the season the neighbouring heights of Altobispo were occupied weekly by the brigades of the division; but as the cold increased with the high winds, the pickets alone were appointed for this duty. Such was the inclemency of the weather, and natural advantages of this position, that it was scarcely thought that the enemy would attempt an attack. This opinion, however, was ill founded, as upon the night of the 11th of October an attempt was made by a strong party upon the advance, composed of 15 men of the Seventy-first, under Sergeant James Ross. Instead of flinching from an unequal contest, this small band, relying upon the strength of the position, and being, moreover, favoured by the darkness, which concealed its strength, maintained its ground, and forced the enemy to retire. The bravery of this party called forth high praise from Lieut.-General the Honourable Sir William Stewart, commanding the division, and at his request the soldiers composing it were all presented with medals.

On the 8th of November the division was again in motion, for the purpose of entering the French territory; and on the 9th of that month it bivouacked near the heights of Maya, where orders were received to march as

1813. light as possible. The heights were passed that night by moonlight for the purpose of joining the grand army; but the march over bad roads was so fatiguing that when the brigade arrived in position on the Nivelle it was not called upon to take an active part in the glorious proceedings of the rest of the army on the 10th of November, in forcing the French from their fortified position on that river.

After the battle of the Nivelle, the battalion marched in the direction of Cambo, on the Nive, where some smart skirmishing occurred, in which 2 men were killed, and 4 sergeants, 1 bugler, and 41 rank and file wounded. When the French crossed to the right bank, the Seventy-first occupied part of the town of Cambo.

The battalion remained in Cambo for nearly a month, and was here joined by a detachment of 4 sergeants and 82 rank and file, under the command of Lieut. Charles Henderson, from the second battalion, at this period stationed at Glasgow.

On the 9th of December the first battalion was engaged in the passage of the Nive. The left wing of the Seventy-first entered the river, supported by the fire of the right, and reached the opposite bank without experiencing any loss.

The enemy now retired within Bayonne, and the corps of Lieut.-General Sir Rowland Hill was established with its right on the Adour, the left above the Nive, and the centre at St. Pierre, across the high road to St. Jean Pied-de-Port.

In this disposition the second division, of which the Seventy-first formed part, was placed at St. Pierre. Marshal Soult, having completely failed in an attempt which he made against the left of the army, moved with his whole force against Sir Rowland Hill's corps, with the expectation of overwhelming him before he could be supported.

The enemy came on with great boldness upon the 13th of December, and made vigorous efforts against the centre, which he repeatedly attacked; but at last, finding his most earnest endeavours fruitless, he drew off. In the action of this day the loss of the first battalion of the Seventy-first was very severe, having been placed close to the main road, against which the French made such formidable and repeated attacks.

1813.

Brevet Lieut.-Colonel Maxwell Mackenzie and Lieutenants William Campbell and Charles Henderson, together with 2 sergeants, 1 bugler, and 23 rank and file, were killed. Captains Robert Barclay and William Alexander Grant, and Lieutenants John M*c*Intyre and William Torriano, with 37 rank and file, were wounded.

The following short, but highly expressive Division Order was issued by Lieut.-General the Honourable Sir William Stewart, K.B.

"*Head-quarters, near Petite Moguerre,*
"*December* 14*th,* 1813.

" The second division has greatly distinguished itself,
" and its gallantry in yesterday's action is avowed by the
" Commander of the Forces and the Allied Army."

In commemoration of these services, the Seventy-first subsequently received the royal authority to bear the word " Nive" on the regimental colour and appointments.

The battalion marched on the 19th of December to Urcuit, and to Urt upon the 28th of that month. A small picket of the Seventy-first, under the command of Corporal Dogherty, here distinguished itself by beating off an enemy's party of nearly treble its strength.

While stationed in this quarter, the companies were frequently engaged in skirmishes with the enemy, particularly at St. Hellette, heights of Garris, and St. Palais, in the month of January, 1814.

1814.

1814. In the beginning of February the battalion marched from Urt, and during its advance had frequent skirmishes with the enemy's rear guard.

On the 26th of February the battalion was in action at Sauveterre, and upon the 27th had the honour of participating in the battle of Orthes.

In commemoration of this victory, the Seventy-first afterwards received the royal authority to bear the word "Orthes" on the regimental colour and appointments.

Two divisions of the French army having retired to Aire after the action of the 27th of February, Lieut.-General Sir Rowland Hill moved upon that town to dislodge them. Upon the 2nd of March the French were found strongly posted upon a ridge of hills, extending across the great road in front of the town, having their right on the Adour. The second division attacked them along the road, seconded by a Portuguese brigade, and drove them from their position. Lieut. James Anderson and 17 rank and file were killed; Lieut. Henry Frederick Lockyer, 1 sergeant, and 19 rank and file were wounded.

A detachment from the second battalion, consisting of 1 captain, 4 subalterns, and 134 rank and file, under the command of Major Arthur Jones, joined at Aire.

On the 25th of March, part of the battalion was engaged in an affair at Tarbes, in which Lieutenant Robert Law was wounded, and upon the 10th of April was in position at Toulouse, where some of the companies were employed skirmishing, and sustained a loss of 1 sergeant and 3 rank and file killed; 6 rank and file were wounded.

During the night of the 11th of April, the French troops evacuated Toulouse, and a white flag was hoisted. On the following day, the Marquis of Wellington entered the city, amidst the acclamations of the inhabitants. In the course of the afternoon of the 13th of April, intelligence was received of the abdication of Napoleon, and had not 1814. the express been delayed on the journey by the French police, the sacrifice of many valuable lives would have been prevented.

A disbelief in the truth of this intelligence occasioned much unnecessary bloodshed at Bayonne, the garrison of which made a desperate sortie on the 14th of April, and Lieutenant Sir John Hope (afterwards Earl of Hopetoun) was taken prisoner. Major-General Andrew Hay was killed, and Major-General Stopford was wounded.

A treaty of peace was established between Great Britain and France; Louis XVIII was restored to the throne of France, and Napoleon Bonaparte was permitted to reside at Elba, the sovereignty of that island having been conceded to him by the Allied Powers.

The war being ended, the first battalion of the Seventy-first regiment marched from Toulouse to Blanchfort, where it was encamped for 16 days, and afterwards proceeded to Pouillac, where it embarked on the 15th of July for England, on board of His Majesty's ship "Sultan" of seventy-four guns.

Prior to the breaking up of the Peninsula army, the Duke of Wellington issued the following General Order:—

"*Bordeaux*, 14*th June*, 1814.

" GENERAL ORDER.

" The Commander of the Forces, being upon the point
" of returning to England, again takes this opportunity of
" congratulating the army upon the recent events which
" have restored peace to their country and to the world.

" The share which the British army have had in pro-
" ducing those events, and the high character with which
" the army will quit this country, must be equally satis-
" factory to every individual belonging to it, as they are to

1814. " the Commander of the Forces, and he trusts that the " troops will continue the same good conduct to the last.

" The Commander of the Forces once more requests " the army to accept his thanks.

" Although circumstances may alter the relations in " which he has stood towards them for some years so much " to his satisfaction, he assures them he will never cease to " feel the warmest interest in their welfare and honour, " and that he will be at all times happy to be of any " service to those to whose conduct, discipline, and gal- " lantry their country is so much indebted."

In addition to the other distinctions acquired during the war in Spain, Portugal, and the South of France, the Seventy-first subsequently received the Royal Authority to bear the word "Peninsula" on the regimental colours and appointments.

The first battalion arrived at Cork on the 28th of July, and marched to Mallow, where it remained for a few days. On the 4th of August, the battalion marched to Limerick, where Colonel Reynell assumed command of it in December, and in which city it continued to be quartered during the remainder of the year.

2nd bat. The second battalion remained stationed in North Britain.

1815. In January, 1815, the first battalion of the Seventy-first
1st bat. regiment marched from Limerick to Cork, and embarked as part of an expedition under orders for North America. Peace having been concluded with the United States, and contrary winds having prevented the sailing of the vessels, the destination of the battalion was changed, and subsequent events occasioned its being employed against its former opponents. The tranquillity which Europe appeared to have gained by the splendid successes over the French in the Peninsula was again to be disturbed. Napoleon, who had been accustomed to imperial sway,

was naturally discontented with his small sovereignty of Elba. Besides, the correspondence kept up by him with his adherents in France, gave him hopes of regaining his former power, which were, for a short time, fully realised. He landed at Cannes in Provence, on the 1st of March, 1815, with a small body of men, and on the 20th of that month entered Paris at the head of an army which had joined him on the road. This could not be wondered at, for the officers and soldiers had won their fame under his command, and gladly welcomed their former leader, under whom they probably expected to acquire fresh honours, which might erase the memory of the defeats sustained in the Peninsula.

Louis XVIII, unable to stem the torrent, withdrew from Paris to Ghent, and Napoleon resumed his former dignity of Emperor of the French. This assumption the Allied Powers determined not to acknowledge, but resolved to deprive him of his sovereignty, and again restore the ancient dynasty.

The first battalion of the Seventy-first, in consequence of these occurrences, proceeded to the Downs, and was there embarked on board small vessels, which conveyed it to Ostend, where it disembarked on the 22nd of April.

The battalion next proceeded to Ghent, and, after remaining there a week, marched to Leuze, between Ath and Fournay, and was subsequently placed in the light brigade with the first battalion of the Fifty-second, six companies of the second, and two companies of the third battalion of the Ninety-fifth Regiment (Rifles), under the command of Major-General Frederick Adam, in the division of Lieut.-General Sir Henry Clinton.

The strength of the brigade was as follows :—

1815.

			Rank and File.
52nd Regt.	1st bat.	...	997
71st do.	do.	...	788
95th do.	2nd bat. Rifles ...	...	571
95th do.	3rd do. do. ...	...	185
	Total	...	2,541

Brevet Colonel Reynell, afterwards Lieut.-General Sir Thomas Reynell, commanded the battalion at this period.

Napoleon resolved on attacking the Allies before their forces had been fully collected, and by well-marked and admirably combined movements, a portion of his army was concentrated, on the 14th of June, between the Sambre and the Meuse.

On the morning of the 16th of June, as the battalion was proceeding to the usual exercising-ground of the brigade at Leuze, it received orders for an immediate advance upon Nivelles, where it arrived late that night. On the same day, Prince Blücher had been attacked at Ligny, and was forced to retreat to Havre. The Duke of Wellington and a portion of his army had been also attacked at Quatre Bras by Marshal Ney, who, however, made no impression upon the British position.

In the course of the morning of the 17th of June, the Duke of Wellington made a retrograde movement upon Waterloo, in order to keep up his communication with the Prussians. At day-break on the same morning, the first battalion of the Seventy-first retired, and took up its position, with the rest of the allied army, on the plains in the neighbourhood of Waterloo, being situated to the left and rear of Hougomont.

The Seventy-first, with the rest of the army, bivouacked in position during the night of the 17th of June, drenched by the rain, which fell heavily. Upon the morning of the memorable 18th of June, the battalion stood in open column, and in this situation was exposed for some time to a heavy fire of artillery, but a judicious movement to a short distance alleviated in a great measure this annoyance. Line was next formed, and about two o'clock the battalion, with the rest of the brigade, advanced, met their opponents in position, charged, and instantly overthrew them.

1815.

A heavy fire now commenced upon the retreating enemy, but the alignment having been completely deranged by the impetuosity of the advance, Colonel Reynell, with his usual coolness, proceeded to restore order, and had just completed the dressing of the line when the French cavalry was seen advancing. Square was instantly formed, and the Seventy-first, with the rest of the brigade, sustained a charge from 3 regiments of French cavalry, namely, 1 of cuirassiers, 1 of grenadiers-à-cheval, and 1 of lancers.

The charge was made with the most obstinate bravery, but nothing could overcome the steadiness of the British infantry, and after a destructive loss, the French were forced to retire. At this moment a piper played up the Seventy-first quick march, followed with the charge. Major-General Adams with the regiment exclaimed, " Well done, Seventy-first; you are all lions together, and " as for you, piper, you are an honour to your country. " Forward, my lads, and give them the charge in style, " as I know and see you can do."

Previously to this advance of the enemy's cavalry the square of the Seventy-first was struck by a round shot, which killed or wounded an officer and 18 men of the eighth company.

About seven o'clock in the evening the left wing of the battalion was formed in rear of the right, and while thus placed was, with the rest of the division, attacked by a column of the Imperial Young Guard, which had been

1815. kept in reserve during the day. It was allowed to approach close without molestation, when the regiments, throwing in a close and well-directed fire, prevented its deployment, and it retired in confusion.

The enemy having now exhausted all its efforts, the British, in their turn, advanced. The Seventy-first, in the first instance, suffered much from the fire of some guns that enfiladed its front; these were soon silenced, and the battalion was afterwards left unmolested. In this advance the light brigade captured several guns. Night closed in fast, and the corps rested after this lengthened and sanguinary encounter, the pursuit of the discomfited enemy being commited to the Prussians, under Marshal Blucher, who had arrived on the field of battle in time to decide the defeat of the French.

The Seventy-first had Brevet Major Edmund L'Estrange (Aide-de-Camp to Major-General Sir Denis Pack, K.C.B.), and Ensign John Todd, killed. The following officers were wounded: the Lieut.-Colonel commanding the battalion, Colonel Thomas Reynell; Brevet Lieut.-Colonel Arthur Jones; Captains Samuel Reed, Donald Campbell, William Alexander Grant, James Henderson, and Brevet Major Charles Johnstone; Lieutenants Joseph Barrallier, Robert Lind, John Roberts, James Coates, Robert Law, Carique Lewin, and Lieutenant and Adjutant William Anderson.

The number of serjeants, buglers, and rank and file killed amounted to 29; 166 were wounded, of whom 36 died of their wounds.

The following were present with the regiment at this battle:—

Colonel, Lieut.-Colonel J. Reynell.
Lieut.-Colonel, Major A. Jones.
Major, L. Walker.

Captains.   1815.

S. Reed.
J. T. Pidgeon.
A. Armstrong.
D. Campbell.
William A. Grant.

J. Henderson.
A. T. M. McIntyre.
C. Johnstone.
Alex. Grant.

Lieutenants.

J. Barrallier.
L. Richards.
J. R. Elwes.
C. Stewart.
R. Baldwin.
W. C. Hanson.
Robert Lind.
J. Roberts.
James Coates.
James Fraser.
E. Gilborne.
J. Whitney.

William Long.
Robert Law.
C. J. Cox.
Carique Lewin.
William Woolcombe.
William Torriano.
G. W. Horton.
J. Coote.
C. Moorhead.
D. Soutar.
N. Campbell.

Ensigns.

A. Moffatt.
W. P. Smith.
H. W. Thompors.
J. Barnett.

A. M. Henderson.
J. Spalding.
J. Impitt.
R. L'Estrange.

Paymaster, H. McKenzie.
Adjutant, William Anderson.
Surgeon, A. Stewart.

Assistant Surgeons.

J. Winterscale. | Samuel Hill.

Both Houses of Parliament, with the greatest enthusiasm, voted their thanks to the army for its " distinguished " valour at Waterloo."

1815. For the share which the battalion had in this glorious victory, the Seventy-first were permitted to bear, in common with the rest of the army engaged upon the 18th of June, the word "Waterloo" on the regimental colour and appointments. Colonel Thomas Reynell and Major L. Walker were appointed Companions of the Bath. The officers and men engaged were presented with silver medals by His Royal Highness the Prince Regent, and were allowed to reckon two years additional service.

The battalion, with the rest of the army, afterwards marched towards Paris, and entered that city on the 7th of July. The brigade encamped that day on the Champs Elysées, near the Place Louis Quinze, being the only British troops quartered within the barriers, and continued there until the beginning of November, when it proceeded to Versailles, and to Viarmes in December.

Meanwhile Louis XVIII had entered Paris and was again reinstated on the throne of his ancestors. Napoleon Bonaparte had surrendered to Captain Maitland, commanding the "Bellerophon," British ship of war, and the island of St. Helena having been fixed for his residence, he was conveyed thither with a few of his devoted followers.

In Edinburgh, on the 26th of July, at the annual competition for prizes given by the Highland Society of London, Sir John Sinclair, President of the Judges, in the course of his address referred to several instances where the sound of the bagpipes had been productive of the most decisive results, and stated that it had been used with the same effect in the late glorious conflicts, as appeared by letters from the army. He said that before he obeyed the directions of the Committee in delivering the prizes it was necessary to state that George Clark, piper-major to the Seventy-first Regiment, having formerly received a pipe from the Highland Society of Scotland for his gallant conduct at the battle of Vimiera in continuing to play upon his pipes after he was severely wounded, it was thought proper to vote him a gold medal instead of considering him as a candidate for one of the prizes.

On the 24th of December, 1815, the second battalion of the Seventy-first was disbanded at Glasgow, the effective officers and men being transferred to the first battalion.

In January, 1816, the Seventy-first marched to the Pas-de-Calais, in which part of France the regiment was quartered in several villages, having its head-quarters at Norrent Fonte, a village on the high road from Calais to Douay.

On the 21st of June, 1816, the regiment assembled on the bruyère of Rombly, between the villages of Lingham and Rombly on the one side, and Viterness and Leitre on the other, for the purpose of receiving the medals which had been granted by His Royal Highness the Prince Regent to the officers, non-commissioned officers, buglers, and privates, for their services at the battle of Waterloo.

A hollow square upon the centre was formed on this occasion; the ranks were opened, and the boxes containing the medals were placed within the square. Colonel Reynell then addressed the regiment in the following manner:—

" Seventy-first!!

" The deep interest, which you will all give me credit
" for feeling, in everything that affects the corps cannot fail
" to be awakened upon an occasion such as the present,
" when holding in my hands, to transfer to yours, these
" honourable rewards bestowed by your Sovereign for your
" share in the great and glorious exertions of the army of
" His Grace the Duke of Wellington upon the field of
" Waterloo, when the utmost efforts of the army of France,
" directed by Napoleon, reputed to be the first captain of

1816. "the age, were not only paralyzed at the moment, but "blasted beyond the power of even a second struggle.

"To have participated in a contest crowned with victory "so decisive, and productive of consequences that have dif-"fused peace, security, and happiness throughout Europe, "may be to each of you a source of honourable pride, as "well as of gratitude to the Omnipotent Arbiter of all "human contests, who preserved you in such peril, and "without whose protecting hand the battle belongs not "to the strong, nor the race to the swift.

"I acknowledge to feel an honest and, I trust, an "excusable, exultation, in having had the honour to com-"mand you on that day, and in dispensing these medals "destined to record in your families the share you had in "the ever memorable battle of Waterloo, it is a peculiar "satisfaction to me that I can present them to those by "whom they have been fairly and honourably earned, and "that I can here solemnly declare that in the course of that "eventful day I did not observe a soldier of this good "regiment whose conduct was not only creditable to the "English nation, but such as his dearest friends could "desire.

"Under such agreeable reflections, I request you to "accept these medals, and to wear them with becoming "pride, as they are incontestable proofs of a faithful dis-"charge of your duty to your King and your country. I "trust that they will act as powerful talismans to keep you "in your future lives in the paths of honour, sobriety, and "virtue."

At the conclusion of the above address the arms were presented, "God save the King" was played, and the battalion, by signal, gave three cheers. Colonel Reynell then, from the lists of companies in succession, called over the names of those entitled to receive a medal, and with his own hand placed it in that of the soldier.

New colours were presented to the regiment on the 18th of January, 1817, by Major-General Sir Denis Pack, K.C.B., who made the following address on the occasion :—

18th 1817.

"Seventy-first Regiment!

"Officers, non-commissioned officers, and soldiers, it "affords me the greatest satisfaction, at the request of "your commanding officer, Colonel Reynell, to have the "honour of presenting these colours to you.

"There are many who could perform the office with a "better grace, but there is no one, believe me, who is more "sensible of the merit of the corps, or who is more anxious "for its honour and welfare.

"I might justly pay to the valour and good conduct of "those present the compliments usual on such occasions, "but I had rather offer the expression of my regard and "admiration of that excellent *esprit de corps* and real worth "which a ten years' intimate knowledge of the regiment "has taught me so highly to appreciate. I shall always "look back with pleasure to that long period in which I "had the good fortune to be your commanding officer, and "during which time I received from the officers the most "cordial and zealous assistance in support of discipline: "from the non-commissioned officers proofs of the most "disinterested regard for His Majesty's service and the "welfare of their regiment, and I witnessed on the part of "the privates and the corps at large a fidelity to their "colours in South America, as remarkable under such "trying circumstances as their valour has at all times been "conspicuous in the field. I am most happy to think that "there is no drawback to the pleasure all should feel on "this occasion. Your former colours were mislaid after a "fête given in London to celebrate the Duke of Welling-"ton's return after his glorious termination of the Peninsula "war, and your colonel, General Francis Dundas, has "sent you three very handsome ones to replace them.

1817. "On them are emblazoned some of His Grace's vic-
"tories, in which the Seventy-first bore a most distinguished
"part, and more might be enumerated which the corps may
"well be proud of. There are still in your ranks valuable
"officers who have witnessed the early glories of the regi-
"ment in the East, and its splendid career since is fresh in
"the memory of all. Never, indeed, did the character of
"the corps stand higher; never was the fame of the British
"arms or the glory of the British empire more prominent
"than at this moment, an enthusiastic recollection of which
"the sight of these colours must always inspire.

"While you have your present commanding officer to
"lead you, it is unnecessary for me to add anything to
"excite such a spirit; but was I called upon to do so, I
"should have only to hold up the example of those who
"have fallen in your ranks, and, above all, point to the
"memory of that hero who so gloriously fell at your
"head."

The following appears from the Regimental Records to be a correct list of the nationalities of the recruits raised for the regiment between 1804 and 1815:—Scotchmen, 2,560; Irishmen, 1,087; Englishmen, 248; foreigners, 20: total, 3,915. The following is the list of casualties sustained by the regiment between 1808 and 1815.

This list is very inaccurate, as no notice is taken in the Records of the number of men that were killed in skirmishes, which probably was very considerable. At Corunna it is stated that several men were killed and wounded, but the actual number is not given. The number of wounded at Walcheren is not given:—

SEVENTY-FIRST HIGHLAND LIGHT INFANTRY.

1817.

Total Killed and Wounded.	Action.	Killed				Wounded			
		Officers.	Sergeants.	Buglers.	Privates.	Officers.	Sergeants.	Buglers.	Privates.
3	Roleia	...	...	...	1	...	...	...	2
112	Vimiera	...	...	...	12	...	6	...	86
1	Corunna	...	...	...	...	...	...	...	...
22	Walcheren	...	...	...	...	1	...	...	...
42	Sobral	2	...	...	19	1	...	...	34
147	Fuentes d'Onor	...	4	...	8	...	6	...	100
43	Almaraz	1	1	...	22	8	3	3	29
13	Alba de Tormes	...	1	...	7	2	1	...	5
370	Vittoria	4	6	1	78	11	13	2	255
140	Maya	...	3	...	54	...	6	1	76
61	Eguaros	1	1	...	23	...	2	1	33
85	Doña Maria	...	...	...	29	8	2	...	45
48	Cambo	...	2	1	2	...	4	...	41
70	Nive	3	...	...	23	4	...	1	37
39	Orthes	1	...	...	17	1	1	...	19
1	Tarbes	...	...	...	...	1	...	...	...
10	Toulouse	...	1	...	3	...	...	...	6
212	Waterloo (killed and died of wounds)	3	3	2	62	14	7	3	120
1,419		19	23	2	366	59	51	11	888

Two officers were taken prisoners at Fuentes d'Onor, and several privates at Orthes. Three men were missing at Waterloo.

II

1818. The regiment formed part of the "army of occupation" in France until towards the end of October, 1818, when it embarked at Calais for England, and arrived at Dover on the 29th of that month.

After landing the regiment proceeded immediately to Chelmsford, where it remained for a short time. During its stay at this place the establishment was reduced from 810 to 650 rank and file.

On the 25th of November the regiment marched to Weedon, Derby, and Nottingham, having its head-quarters at the former place.

1819. The regiment was inspected at Weedon on the 1st of May, 1819, by Major-General Sir John Byng, who reported most favourably to His Royal Highness the Commander-in-Chief upon its appearance and discipline. In consequence of this report His Royal Highness was pleased to dispense with any further inspection of the regiment during the year.

Whilst stationed at Weedon, Colonel Reynell presented Sergeant Angus Mackay, Pipe Major, with a highland purse of white goat-skin handsomely mounted with silver, with the following inscription richly engraved on a shield :—

" From Col. Reynell to Acting-Sergeant Angus Mackay, " Piper in the Seventy-first H.L.I., in testimony of appro- " bation of his uniform good conduct."

On the 21st of June, 1819, the regiment marched to Chester, having detachments at Liverpool and the Isle of Man. On August 12th, Colonel Thomas Reynell was appointed Major-General by brevet.

1820. In June, 1820, the regiment marched to Rochdale, Blackburn, and Burnley. In July following it proceeded to Hertford, Ware, Hoddesdon, and Hatfield; and on the 20th of November it was removed to Canterbury.

Previously to the departure of the regiment from Hertford, it was inspected by the Adjutant-General to the

Forces, Major-General Sir Henry Torrens, K.C.B., who 1820. communicated to Colonel Sir Thomas Arbuthnot, K.C.B., commanding the Seventy-first, the expression of the satisfaction experienced by His Royal Highness the Commander-in-Chief in perusing the report made on that occasion.

In June, 1821, the regiment marched to Chatham, 1821. having detachments at Sheerness, Tilbury Fort, and Harwich. Here a further reduction took place of 2 companies, making the establishment to consist of 576 rank and file.

From Chatham the regiment marched to London, and 1822. proceeded by the canal to Liverpool, there to embark for Dublin, where it arrived on the 3rd of May, 1822. The regiment remained in that city until the beginning of October, when it marched to the south of Ireland. The head-quarters were stationed at Fermoy, and detachments proceeded to the villages of Ballyhooly, Castletown Roche, Kilworth, Kildorrery, Wattstown, Glanworth, and Mitchelstown. A subaltern's party was also encamped at Glennasheen, in the county of Limerick, the disturbed state of that part of Ireland requiring detachments in the above posts, and the utmost exertions of every individual for their protection.

Lieut.-General Sir Gordon Drummond, G.C.B., was 1824. removed from the colonelcy of the Eighty-eighth to that of the Seventy-first Regiment, on the 16th of January, 1824, in succession to General Francis Dundas, deceased.

The regiment remained here for two winters, and in the beginning of May, 1824, orders were received to march to the Cove of Cork, to embark for foreign service.

Before the Seventy-first marched to the coast for embarkation, very gratifying addresses were presented to Colonel Sir Thomas Arbuthnot, commanding the regiment, from the magistrates and inhabitants of the district round

1824. Fermoy, conveying their approbation of the conduct of the corps, which had won the esteem of all classes.

A very gratifying order was also issued by Major-General Sir John Lambert, K.C.B., commanding the south-western district of Ireland, relative to the conduct of the regiment. The regiment embarked for North America on the 14th, 16th, 17th, and 18th of May, 1824, on board the Indian trader "Prince of Orange," "Cato" and "Fanny" transports, and anchored at Quebec, on the 23rd, 24th, and 25th of June.

1825. In the year 1825, the establishment of the regiment was augmented from 8 to 10 companies, and formed into 6 *service* and 4 *depôt* companies, consisting of 42 sergeants, 14 buglers, and 740 rank and file.

In consequence of this arrangement, the officers and non-commissioned officers of 2 companies were sent to England, to join the depôt companies at Chichester.

1826. The detachments stationed during the summer months at the posts of Sorel and Three Rivers, rejoined the head quarters of the regiment at Quebec, on the 15th of October.

On the 25th of October and the 4th of November the service companies were inspected by Lieut.-General the Earl of Dalhousie, the Commander of the Forces in British North America, who expressed his fullest approbation of their discipline and interior economy, as well as of their conduct and appearance.

1827. The head-quarter division of the Seventy-first embarked at Quebec for Montreal, on the 17th of May, 1827, after having been stationed in that garrison nearly three years. Preparatory to this change of quarters, the service companies were again inspected by Lieut.-General the Earl of Dalhousie, who, in orders, assured Lieut.-Colonel Jones that he had never seen any regiment in more perfect order.

The service companies arrived at Montreal on the 19th

of May, and detachments from them were stationed at 1827. Isle-aux-Noix, St. John's, William Henry, La Chine, Coteau-du-Lac, and Rideau.

On the 8th of May, 1828, the Seventy-first embarked 1828. for Kingston in batteaux, and arrived there on the 16th of that month. It remained stationed here for 12 months. During the summer and part of the autumn it suffered much from fever and ague, having had at one period nearly a third of the men in hospital.

Upon the 1st of June, 1829, the head-quarters embarked 1829. in a steamboat for York, now called Toronto, the capital of the Upper Province, and arrived there on the following morning. One company was detached to Niagara, another to Amherstburg, and a third to Penetanguishene, on Lake Huron. A small number of men occupied the naval post at Grand River, on Lake Erie. The Seventy-first occupied these posts for a period of two years.

On the 10th of August, 1829, the depôt companies embarked at Gravesend, for Berwick-on-Tweed.

Major-General Sir Colin Halkett, K.C.B., was removed from the colonelcy of the Ninety-fifth to that of the Seventy-first Regiment, on the 21st of September, 1829, in succession to General Sir Gordon Drummond, G.C.B., who was appointed to the Forty-ninth Regiment.

In June, 1830, the depôt companies were removed from 1830. Berwick-on-Tweed to Edinburgh Castle.

In May, 1831, the service companies moved down to 1831. Quebec, where the whole were assembled on the 16th of June. After a stay of nearly five months in that city, orders arrived for them to proceed to Bermuda. They embarked on the 20th of October, 1831, in the transports "Layton" and "Manlins," arriving off St. George's, Bermuda, upon the 11th of November, when they immediately disembarked, sending a detachment of 1 captain, 2 subalterns, and 120 men to Ireland Island.

1831. The head-quarters were subsequently moved to Hamilton, and small parties were detached to the signal posts at Gibbs Hill and Mount Langton.

1833. During the years 1832 and 1833, the service companies continued at Bermuda, and the depôt remained in North Britain. On the 30th of August, 1833, Lieut.-Colonel the Honourable Charles Grey exchanged from the half-pay to the Seventy-first Highlanders with Lieut.-Colonel Joseph Thomas Pidgeon.

1834. On the 11th of September, 1834, the service companies embarked at Bermuda for Great Britain, and arrived at Leith on the 19th of October following. The regiment was afterwards stationed at Edinburgh, where it remained during the year 1835. It embarked at Glasgow, on the

1836. 11th of May, 1836, for Ireland, and was stationed at Dublin during the remainder of the year. New colours were presented to the regiment while at this station, by the colonel of the regiment, Lieut.-General Sir Colin Halkett, K.C.B., K.C.H., assisted by the Honourable Mrs. Grey, wife of the colonel commanding the regiment.

1837. In June, 1837, the regiment proceeded from Dublin to Kilkenny.

1838. Major-General Sir Samuel Ford Whittingham, K.C.B., was appointed Colonel of the Seventy-first Highlanders, on the 28th of March, 1838, in succession to Lieut.-General Sir Colin Halkett, K.C.B., appointed to the Thirty-first Regiment.

Meanwhile orders had been received for the regiment to proceed on foreign service, and on the 20th of April, 1838, the 6 service companies embarked at Cork, for Canada. The 4 depôt companies remained in Ireland.

1839. On the 2nd of June, 1839, the depôt companies embarked at Cork, for North Britain, and were afterwards stationed at Stirling.

The establishment of the regiment was augmented on 1839. the 12th of August, 1839, from 740 to 800 rank and file.

During the year 1840 the service companies were sta- 1840. tioned at St. John's, Lower Canada. The depôt companies proceeded from Stirling to Dundee, in April.

Lieut.-General Sir Thomas Reynell, Bart., K.C.B., was 1841. removed from the colonelcy of the Eighty-seventh Royal Irish Fusiliers to that of the Seventy-first, on the 15th of March, 1841, in succession to Lieut.-General Sir Samuel Ford Whittingham, K.C.B. and K.C.H., deceased.

In May, 1841, the depôt companies proceeded from Dundee to Aberdeen.

Lieut.-Colonel the Honourable Charles Grey exchanged to half-pay with Lieut.-Colonel James England, on the 8th of April, 1842.

The service companies proceeded from St. John's to 1842. Montreal in two divisions, on the 27th and 28th of April, 1842.

In consequence of the augmentation which took place in the army at this period, the Seventy-first Highland Light Infantry was ordered to be divided into two battalions, the six service companies being termed the first battalion, and the depôt, augmented by two new companies, being styled the reserve battalion. The depôt was accordingly moved from Stirling to Chichester, and after receiving about 350 volunteers from other corps, was there organised into a battalion for foreign service. Nearly all these volunteers were English and Irish, who were allowed to join the regiment notwithstanding the protestations of the commanding officer, who requested that none but Scotchmen should be allowed to volunteer. The nationality of the regiment was thereby unnecessarily destroyed for many years.

The reserve battalion of the Seventy-first, under the command of Lieut.-Colonel James England, embarked at

1842. Portsmouth in Her Majesty's troop ship "Resistance," which sailed for Canada on the 13th of August, 1842, and the battalion landed at Montreal on the 23rd of September, where the first battalion was likewise stationed, under the command of Major William Denny, who, upon the arrival of Lieut.-Colonel England, took charge of the reserve battalion.

1843. The reserve battalion marched from Montreal to Chambly on the 5th of May, 1843, and arrived there on the same day.

The first battalion, under the command of Lieut.-Colonel England, embarked at Quebec for the West Indies in the "Java" transport, on the 20th of October, 1843. The head-quarters disembarked at Grenada on the 15th of December following.

It is a circumstance worthy of record that all the men of the first battalion who were married without leave were replaced by volunteers from the reserve battalion, thereby preventing the separation and consequent misery of those families, and that all permanent volunteers for Canada, and old soldiers who were permitted from general good character to remain in the colony after discharge, or who were found unfit for service in a tropical climate, were replaced by volunteers from the reserve battalion.

1844. The head-quarters of the first battalion embarked on the 25th of December, 1844, at Grenada, for Antigua. Lieut. Francis P. Stewart Mackenzie died of yellow fever at Grenada, on the 21st of December, much regretted by his brother officers.

1845. During the year 1845 the head-quarters of the first battalion continued at Antigua.

The head-quarters and three companies of the reserve battalion marched from Chambly on the 11th of May, 1845, and arrived at Kingston, in Canada, on the 14th of that month.

On the 18th of April, 1846, the head-quarters and four companies of the first battalion embarked at Antigua, on board the transport "Princess Royal," and landed at Barbadoes on the 24th of the same month. 1846.

The first battalion, under the command of Captain Nathaniel Massey Stack, embarked for England at Barbadoes on the 29th and 31st of December, on board of Her Majesty's ship "Belleisle." During this tour of service in the West Indies, which lasted just three years, 1 officer, 8 sergeants, and 124 rank and file died of fever and dysentery.

On the 6th of October, 1846, the reserve battalion left Kingston, in Canada West, and the head-quarters arrived at La Prairie on the 8th of that month.

The ship "Belleisle," having the first battalion on board, sailed for Portsmouth on the 1st of January, 1847, and arrived at Spithead on the 25th of that month. After disembarking at Portsmouth, the battalion proceeded to Winchester, where it was stationed until the 19th of July, when it was conveyed in three divisions by railway to Glasgow, and on the 21st of December it was removed to Edinburgh. 1847.

In September, 1847, the head-quarters of the reserve battalion were removed from La Prairie to Chambly, and in October proceeded to St. John's, in Canada East.

Lieutenant-General Sir Thomas Arbuthnot, K.C.B., was removed from the colonelcy of the Ninth Foot to that of the Seventy-first Highlanders on the 18th of February, 1848, in succession to Lieut.-General Sir Thomas Reynell, Bart. and K.C.B., deceased. 1848

Three companies of the first battalion proceeded from Edinburgh to Dublin on the 27th of April, 1848, and the head-quarters, with the three remaining companies, were removed to Dublin on the 1st of May. In June the head-quarters were removed to Naas.

1848. During the year 1848, the head-quarters of the reserve battalion remained at St. John's, in Canada East.

1849. Lieut.-General Sir James Macdonell, K.C.B. and K.C.H., was appointed from the Seventy-ninth to be Colonel of the Seventy-first on the 8th of February, 1849, upon the decease of Lieut.-General Sir Thomas Arbuthnot, K.C.B.

In compliance with instructions received upon the occasion of Her Majesty's visit to Dublin, the head-quarters of the first battalion, with the effectives of three companies, proceeded from Naas to that garrison on the 28th of July, and were encamped in the Phœnix Park. The three detached companies also joined at the encampment on the same day. On the 13th of August the head-quarters and three companies returned to Naas.

The head-quarters and two companies of the reserve battalion, under the command of Lieut.-Colonel Sir Hew Dalrymple, Bart., proceeded from St. John's to Montreal, in aid of the civil power, on the 28th of April, 1849. The head-quarters and three companies quitted Montreal, and encamped on the island of St. Helen's on the 30th of June, but returned to St. John's on the 16th of July. On the 17th of August, 1849, the head-quarters and two companies proceeded from St. John's to Montreal in aid of the civil power, and returned to St. John's on the 6th of September.

1850. In April, 1850, the first battalion proceeded from Naas to Dublin.

The head-quarters and two companies of the reserve battalion quitted St. John's and Chambly on the 21st of May, 1850, and arrived at Toronto on the 23rd of that month, where the battalion was joined by the other companies, and it continued there during the remainder of the year.

1851. In April, 1851, the first battalion proceeded from Dublin

to Mullingar, and in July following was removed to Newry, **1851.**
under the command of Lieut.-Colonel William Denny.

During the year 1851, the reserve battalion continued to be stationed at Toronto.

In May, 1852, the reserve battalion proceeded from **1852.**
Toronto to Kingston. On the 8th of June following, Lieut.-Colonel Sir Hew Dalrymple, Bart., retired from the service by the sale of his commission, and was succeeded by Lieut.-Colonel Nathaniel Massey Stack.

In August the first battalion moved to Kilkenny, sending detachments to New Ross and Wexford.

On the 1st of November orders were received from the Horse Guards by the first battalion to hold itself in readiness for embarkation for the Mediterranean.

On the 3rd of January it received new colours, shortly **1853.**
after which it moved to Cork. Soon after the arrival of the first battalion at Cork, the old colours were placed over a tablet erected at Kinsale to the memory of the late Lieut.-General Sir Thomas Arbuthnot, a native of that place, who commanded the regiment for many years.

During the months of February and March the first battalion embarked in three freight ships for Corfu. By a War Office Letter of 20th February, 1854, the first battalion was augmented from the 1st April by 1 pipe major and 5 pipers. In May, 1853, the reserve battalion proceeded to Quebec, and was quartered in the Citadel. After the embarkation of the first battalion, the depôt proceeded to Chatham.

The reserve battalion embarked at Quebec on the 20th September, landed in England on the 13th of October, and proceeded to Canterbury, where it was shortly afterwards joined by the depôt from Chatham. On its departure from Canada, 100 men volunteered to the Sixteenth and Canadian Rifles. On the 1st of January of this year the following was the composition of

1854. the first and reserve battalion. The depôt is not included :—

	Scotch.	English.	Irish.	Total.	Presbyterians.	Church of England.	Church of Rome.
1st battalion	540	21	34	595	517	37	41
Reserve battalion	470	38	26	534	467	34	33
Total	1,010	59	60	1,129	984	71	74

The English and Irish were all, with the exception of boys from the Military Colleges, the remains of the volunteers who joined the reserve battalion in 1842. On the 24th of November, all the effectives of the reserve battalion, consisting of 1 major, 3 captains, 6 subalterns, 1 assistant surgeon, 20 sergeants, 6 buglers, and 391 rank and file, embarked at Portsmouth on board the line-of-battle ship "Royal Albert," for the Crimea, and landed at Balaclava on the 20th of December, where it was kept, sending frequent working parties to the front. The reserve battalion thus had six weeks' home service after being twelve years abroad.

1855. The first battalion embarked at Corfu for the Crimea on board the transport "Medway" on the 26th January, 1855, and landed at Balaclava on the 7th of February. On the 13th the first and reserve battalions were amalgamated into one battalion of eight companies, about 900 strong, of all ranks. It remained at Balaclava till the 3rd of May, when it embarked on board the "Furious" and "Gladiator" steam frigates, forming part of the first expedition to Kertch, which, however, was recalled without accomplishing its object. The regiment was disembarked on the 8th of May, and marched to the front, joining the third brigade of the fourth division, and serving in the trenches. It was re-embarked on board the frigates 1855. "Sidon" and "Valorous" on the 22nd of May, and proceeded to Kertch with the expeditionary force of the Allied army. The whole landed at Kamish Burnu (about five miles from Kertch), under cover of the gunboats, bivouacked that night, and proceeded the next day, marching through Kertch to Yenikale, where it encamped. The regiment re-embarked at Yenikale on the 10th of June, on board the steam frigates "Sidon" and "Valorous," to return to Sebastopol, but was again disembarked on the 12th, the head-quarters and right wing remaining at Yenikale, and the left wing proceeding to Cape St. Paul, to protect those points in conjunction with a French and Turkish force.

In the beginning of August a draft of 120 men, under Captain Rich, disembarked at Balaclava, and marched to the front. It was attached to the Highland division, being occasionally employed in the trenches. At the end of September it embarked for Yenikale, and joined the head-quarters on the 2nd of October. On the 24th of September three companies, under Major Hunter, crossed the Straits of Yenikale, in conjunction with a French force, to Taman, where a large quantity of hutting material and fuel was obtained. The expedition returned to Kertch on the 3rd of October.

The strength and composition of the regiment on the 1856. 1st of January was as follows, exclusive of a depôt at Malta, which was about 100 strong :—

	Scotch.	English.	Irish.	Total.
Head-quarters ...	823	36	44	903
Depôt at Perth	264	37	50	351
Total	1,087	73	94	1,254

1856. of which, Presbyterians 1,061, Church of England 77, Church of Rome 116.

The head-quarters and six companies, under Colonel Ready, remained in Yenikale, having two companies on detachment, under Major Campbell, at Kertch, till the 30th of May, when the head-quarters moved into Kertch, which was handed over to the Russian authorities on the 22nd of June. On the same day the head-quarters and six companies embarked on board the steam ship "Pacific," and two under Major Campbell, in the steam ship "Edina," and disembarked at Malta on the 29th of June.

The Highland brigade having been kept in reserve during the war, had few casualties in proportion to other regiments. The Seventy-first had only 2 men killed, 6 wounded, and 1 taken prisoner. Major K. Hunter, Lieut. Northey, Assistant-Surgeon Gilborne, and about 100 non-commissioned officers and men died of sickness. The regiment whilst stationed at Malta occupied the Floriana, Ricasoli, and Verdala Barracks.

1857. On the 1st of January, 1857, the following was the strength and composition of the regiment:—

Nationality.	English.	Irish.	Scotch.	Total.
Head-quarters	32	47	795	874
Depôt at Perth	25	37	290	352
Total	57	84	1,085	1,226

of which, 1,043 Presbyterians, 67 Church of England, and 116 Church of Rome.

On the 26th of November, a draft of 2 officers and 41 men joined the head-quarters from the depôt.

1858. On the evening of the 2nd of January, 1858, the regiment received orders by telegram to proceed overland to India. The head-quarters and six companies, under Lieut.-

SEVENTY-FIRST HIGHLAND LIGHT INFANTRY. 127

Colonel Campbell, embarked on board the line-of-battle ship "Princess Royal," on the 4th, 36 hours later, and disembarked at Alexandria on the 18th. Two companies, under Major Hope, which proceeded in Her Majesty's ship "Vulture," disembarked there a few days previously. The regiment then proceeded in two divisions, by railway, to a place half way between Cairo and Suez, where they were mounted on donkeys, and proceeded to Suez, a distance of about 20 or 25 miles. Owing to the smallness of the donkeys, and the size of many of the men, most of them preferred marching to riding. The head-quarters and right wing, under command of Lieut.-Colonel Campbell, arrived at Bombay on the 6th of February, and proceeded to Mhow by bullock train in several detachments, the last of which arrived on the 17th of March. The whole marched from Mhow on the 30th of March, to join the Central India Field Force, under Major-General Sir Hugh Rose, K.C.B. They joined the second brigade at Moti on the 3rd of May, were present at the action of Koonch on the 7th of May, the actions at Muttra and Deapoora on the 16th and 17th of May, action at Golowlee on the 22nd of May, occupation of Calpee on the 23rd of May. This wing was also present at the action of Morar on the 16th of June, on which occasion Lieut. Wyndham Neave, 1 sergeant, 1 corporal, and 2 privates were killed and 8 privates wounded. Private George Rodgers was granted the Victoria Cross for distinguished conduct and courage on this occasion. Lieut.-Colonel Campbell, Major Rich, and Lieut. Scott were especially mentioned.

On the 19th and 20th the whole force, in conjunction with Brigadier Smith's column, took possession of Gwalior. Great sufferings from the excessive heat were undergone by the Central India Force, all the actions having taken place in the two hottest months of an Indian summer. To avoid the excessive power of the sun, the marches were

1858.

1858. always, when practicable, conducted at night, but owing to the heat and the plague of flies, but little rest could be got in the daytime, the thermometer in the tents generally standing at 120°. About 50 men of the regiment died of sunstroke on the march, and many died soon after arrival at Morar from utter exhaustion and weakness.

After the capture of Gwalior the regiment returned to Morar, where it was stationed till the 12th of August, when it returned to Gwalior, and was stationed at the Lashkar
1859. and Phaol Bagh, and returned again to Morar on the 6th of June, 1859. On the 11th of November a small field force, under Lieut.-Colonel Rich, Seventy-first, including a detachment of the Seventy-first, went out into the jungle to look for the rebel forces, and defeated them at Ranode and at Nainwass, on which last occasion 3 privates were killed. This detachment returned to Gwalior on the 27th of May, 1859.

The left wing, which had arrived at Bombay on the 8th of February, started on the 11th of March for Mhow, and arrived there on the 17th of April. On the 9th of June a company was sent to Indore. On the 2nd of September the whole of the detachment in Mhow marched with a field force under command of Major-General Michel, C.B., in pursuit of the rebels, under their celebrated leader Tantia Topee. It was present at the actions at Rajghur, 15th of September, Mongrowlee, 9th of October (on which occasion 1 private was killed), Sindwaho, 19th of October, and Koorai, 25th of October, and afterwards marched to Goonah, where it arrived on the 17th January, 1859. On the 25th of November a party of 50 men, mounted on camels, left Mhow with a small column, under command of Major Sutherland, Ninety-second Highlanders, and was engaged with the rebels at Rajpore on the 25th November, when the latter were defeated, after which they returned to Mhow.

On the 1st of January, 1859, the company which had

been stationed at Indore marched to join a column under Brigadier-General Sir Robert Napier, K.C.B., and was present at the attack on the fort of Nahargurh on the 17th of January, on which occasion 2 privates were severely wounded. Captain F. W. Lambton, in command of the company, was specially mentioned for his daring attack, for which service he was subsequently granted a brevet-majority. Two companies joined head-quarters from Goonah, in June, leaving a detachment of three companies there.

1859.

The head-quarters were inspected on the 2nd of December, 1859, by the Commander-in-Chief, Lord Clyde. His Excellency was pleased to express his satisfaction, both at what he himself saw, and at the reports which he had received regarding the state of the regiment from other sources. The report of His Excellency to His Royal Highness the General Commanding-in-Chief produced the following letter from the Adjutant-General of the Forces.

"*Horse Guards*,
"Sir,   "24*th January*, 1860.

"His Royal Highness the General Commanding-in-
"Chief is much gratified to hear from General Lord
"Clyde, Commander-in-Chief in India, that at his Lord-
"ship's late visit to the station occupied by the regiment
"under your command, he found it in the highest order.
"After the recent arduous and continuous duties on which
"it has been employed, great credit is due to its Com-
"manding Officer and to every rank in the corps, and His
"Royal Highness requests that his opinion may be com-
"municated to them accordingly.

"I have the honour to be, Sir,
"Your most obedient servant,
(Signed)   "G. A. WETHERALL, *General*,
"*Adjutant-General.*

"*Colonel W. Hope,*
"*Commanding Seventy-first Regiment.*"

1859. The three companies on detachment at Goonah rejoined head-quarters on the 19th of December, and the regiment, after being broken up into detachments for two years, was brought together again.

In the month of December Colonel R. D. Campbell died in London, and the command of the regiment devolved on Colonel W. Hope, C.B.

1860. On the 22nd of July cholera broke out in the regiment, and in spite of every sanitary measure being taken, did not finally disappear till the 16th of September, during which time it carried off 1 colour sergeant, 2 sergeants, 66 rank and file, 11 women, and 11 children. It is worthy of remark that during this time only 1 officer was slightly attacked.

On the 20th of December, the regiment having been relieved by the Twenty-seventh Enniskeillens, marched to Sealkote, in the Punjab. The state of discipline of the regiment whilst at Gwalior can be gathered from the following official reports :—

Extract from a Report from the Political Agent at Gwalior to the Government of India, dated 15th June, 1859 :—

" When it was detetmined in June last to post a British
" force at the Laskar, the people expected with dread and
" deprecation a violent and dangerous, at the least a rude
" and overbearing, soldiery ; but Her Majesty's Seventy-
" first Highlanders soon falsified their expectations, and
" created new feelings. His Highness and the best in-
" formed men of the Durbar have assured me that those
" soldiers, who passed ten months in the Phoolbagh,
" have by their manners, habits, dealings, and whole
" demeanour so conciliated the respect and regard of all,
" that nothing could be more acceptable than the domesti ·
" cation of such a force in the capital. The Durbar

"further considers that it would bring to Gwalior incal- 1860.
"culable industrial advantages, through affording a con-
"stant supply of superintendents of public works and
"skilled labour. I venture to express the hope that His
"Excellency may consider the Durbar's view of the con-
"duct of Her Majesty's Seventy-first Highlanders, com-
"manded by Colonel Campbell, C.B., a very high and
"true compliment, as worthy of express recognition as
"good conduct in the field. It is, in my humble judg-
"ment, a most fully deserved compliment.
  (Signed) "A. A. CHARTERS MACPHERSON,
     "*Political Agent.*"

     "*Camp, Agra,*
      "*29th November,* 1859.
"MY LORD,
 "As your Lordship is going to Gwalior, I trust you
"will not think that I exceed my office if I venture to
"send you an extract from a report of June last, in which
"I attract the attention of Government to the admirable
"conduct of Her Majesty's Seventy-first Highlanders,
"and to its appreciation by Maharajah Scindia and his
"people. The importance of such conduct on the part
"of the first British troops stationed at the capital of
"Gwalior might scarcely be over-stated. Having lived
"with the Seventy-first at the Phoolbagh for about twelve
"months, my pride in them as soldiers and countrymen
"must be my excuse to your Lordship for venturing
"upon the irregular communications of my impressions.
 "General Napier's views will, I trust, confirm them.
  (Signed) "A. A. CHARTERS MACPHERSON,
     "*Political Agent.*"

 Extract from remarks by His Royal Highness the

1860. General Commanding-in-Chief, on the Confidential Reports for the year 1859:—

"*Horse Guards,*
"*10th November,* 1860.

"Brigadier-General Sir Robert Napier's Report upon "the Seventy-first Regiment is as satisfactory to His "Royal Highness and as creditable to the corps as it "is excellent in itself.

(Signed) "H. D. TORRENS,
"*Assistant Adjutant-General,*
"*Her Majesty's Forces.*

"*Simla,*
"*1st March,* 1861."

1861. The regiment marched into Sealkote on the 17th of February. The following was the strength and composition of the regiment at this time:—

Nationality.	English.	Scotch.	Irish.	Total.
In India	29	659	43	731
Depôt at Perth	36	177	41	254
Total	65	836	84	985

of which 790 were Presbyterians, 67 Church of England, and 128 Roman Catholics. A draft of 130 men on its way to India is not included. The proportion of English and Irish in the regiment at this time was less than in any other Highland regiment.

1862. The regiment remained stationed at Sealkote till the 1st of November, 1862, when, having been relieved by the Ninety-third Highlanders, it marched to Nowshera, where it arrived on the 21st of November, detaching one company to Attock.

1863. The regiment remained at Nowshera till the 14th of

October, 1863, when, in accordance with instructions re- 1862. ceived from head-quarters, it marched to Nawakilla, in the Yusufzai country, leaving all sick men and invalids behind at Nowshera. The force which was assembled at Nawakilla for service in the hill country was under the command of Brigadier-General Sir Neville Chamberlain, K.C.B. The object of the expedition was to destroy Mulka, on the Mahaban Mountain, the stronghold of certain Hindoostance fanatics, generally known as the "Sitana" fanatics, who infested our frontiers, and were incessantly attacking the villages in our territory. Mulka is just beyond the English frontier, and in the territory of the Indoons. The force marched in two divisions; the first, entirely composed of native troops, marched on the 18th; the second, composed of European troops, marched on the 20th. The Umbeylah Pass was seized without difficulty, but, owing to the bad road, the march, although a comparatively short one, lasted nearly 24 hours, and several days passed before all the guns and baggage were brought up. On the 21st the regiment encamped near the village of Umbeylah. On the 26th of October, 150 men of the Seventy-first, under Major Parker, were engaged in repelling an attack from the enemy, on which occasion 1 private was killed and 5 were wounded. Privates William Clapperton and George Stewart were recommended for the medal for service in the field on this occasion. On the 30th the enemy made another attack on the pickets, but were repulsed. The Seventy-first had 3 privates wounded on this occasion. On the 6th November a party of the regiment was attacked by the enemy, having been sent too far to the front, and not properly supported. Ensign C. B. Murray, Lieut. Dougal, Seventy-ninth, attached, 1 sergeant, and 3 privates were killed, and 4 privates were wounded. Captain Mounsey and Lieut. Davidson, the latter of the Indian Army attached to the Seventy-

1863, first, were specially mentioned for their gallantry on this occasion. On the 18th the whole force changed position to higher ground, and was immediately attacked by the enemy, who was not repulsed before night. On this occasion Captain C. T. Smith, Lieut. Gore Jones, of the Seventy-ninth Highlanders, doing duty with the Seventy-first, and 4 privates, were killed, 1 sergeant and 4 privates were wounded. Major Parker was specially mentioned for his services. On the 19th Captain Aldridge and 1 private were killed; 1 private was wounded. On the 20th, the enemy, having succeeded in driving out the 101st Fusiliers from the "Crag Picket," by a sudden and unexpected attack, the Seventy-first were ordered up to retake it. The "Crag Picket" was situated at the top of a very rocky hill, which rendered the operation doubly difficult. Led by Colonel W. Hope, C.B., who was severely wounded, and supported by two native corps, the Seventy-first, in spite of the natural obstacles and the determined resistance of the enemy, retook the "Crag Picket" at the point of the bayonet. The loss on this occasion was 7 privates killed, 1 field officer, 2 sergeants, 3 corporals, and 19 privates wounded. On the 27th, 1 private was killed. On the 15th of December Major-General Garvoch, commanding the Peshawur division, had succeeded Sir N. Chamberlain in the command of the whole force, when the latter was wounded on the 20th of November. Having received strong reinforcements, he attacked and defeated the enemy on all points. The regiment, being on picket duty, was not engaged on this occasion. Shortly after the Boneyrs asked for and obtained terms of peace. The regiment returned to Nowshera on the 30th December.

The following was the loss sustained by the regiment in the Umbeylah Pass. 5 officers (including Lieutenants Dougal and Jones of the Seventy-ninth attached), 1 sergeant, and 17 privates killed; 1 officer, 4 sergeants, and 42 privates wounded.

1864

On the 4th of January the regiment marched for Peshawur, where it arrived on the 5th. On the 21st of January it was inspected by His Excellency Sir Hugh Rose, K.C.B., who expressed himself in the most complimentary manner with reference to the conduct of the regiment in the late campaign. The three men whose names had appeared in General Orders, Privates William Malcolm, William Clapperton, and George Stewart, were called to the front, and were addressed by His Excellency in terms of approval of their gallant conduct in the presence of the enemy. On the 23rd of October the regiment commenced its march for Calcutta prior to embarkation for England. At Rawal Pindee it was called upon to give volunteers for the other regiments in the Bengal Presidency. 200 men volunteered, and were transferred accordingly. At Umbala, on the 14th of December, at a general parade of the garrison, medals for "gallant conduct in the field" were presented by Major-General Lord George Paget, commanding the Sirhind division, to Sergeant-Major John Blackwood, Privates William Malcolm, William Macdonald, William Clapperton, and George Stewart. Sergeant-Major J. Blackwood, who had been dangerously wounded, was also granted an annuity of £15 a year, and was shortly afterwards invalided on account of his wound. He has since been appointed one of Her Majesty's Yeomen of the Guard and Sergeant-Major of the Second Royal Lanark Militia.

On the 4th of February the head-quarters and right wing under Colonel Hope, C.B., embarked at Calcutta; the left wing, under Major Gore, embarked on the 14th of February.

1865.

The right wing arrived at Plymouth on the 29th of May, and shortly afterwards proceeded to Edinburgh Castle,

1865. where it was joined by the left wing, which disembarked at Gravesend on the 19th of June.

The following divisional and general orders were published before the regiment left India:—

Extract of divisional order by Major-General Sir John Garvock, K.C.B., Commanding Peshawur Division.

"*Rawul Pindee,*
"*1st November,* 1864.

"The Seventy-first Highland Light Infantry being
" about to leave the Peshawur Division *en route* for
" England, the Major-General desires to offer them his best
" wishes on the occasion. He has known the regiment for
" a number of years. He was very intimately associated
" with it in the Mediterranean, and his interest in it is now
" materially increased in no small degree by its having
" served under him in the field, and done its part, and done
" it well, in obtaining for him those honours which Her
" Majesty has been pleased to confer. The Major-General
" had not assumed command of the Yusufzai Field Force
" when the Seventy-first recaptured the 'Crag Picket,'
" but he well knows it was a most gallant exploit. Sir
" John Garvock, K.C.B., begs Colonel Hope, C.B., and the
" officers, non-commissioned officers, and soldiers of the
" Seventy-first Light Infantry to believe that although
" they will be soon no longer under his command, he will
" continue to take the liveliest interest in their career, and
" he now wishes them a speedy and prosperous voyage.

(Signed) "J. WRIGHT, *Lieut.-Colonel,*
"*Assistant Adjutant-General.*"

General order by His Excellency the Commander-in-Chief.

"*Head-quarters, Calcutta,*
"*27th January,* 1865.

"The services of the Seventy-first Highland Light

"Infantry in India entitle them, on their departure to 1865. England, to honourable mention in general orders. A wing of the regiment, on their arrival in India in 1858, joined the Central India Field Force, and His Excellency is enabled to bear testimony to the good services which they performed, and the excellent spirit which they displayed during that campaign. The regiment more recently distinguished itself under their Commanding Officer, Colonel W. Hope, C.B., in the late operations on the frontier. Sir Hugh Rose cannot, in justice to military merit, speak of the Seventy-first in a general order without reverting to an earlier period, when in two great campaigns in Europe they won a reputation which has earned them an honourable page in history.

"Sir Hugh Rose's best wishes attend this distinguished regiment on their leaving his command for home.

"By order of His Excellency the Commander-in-Chief.

(Signed) "G. HAYTHORN, *Colonel*,
"*AdjutantGeneral.*"

The losses of the regiment during the seven years it was quartered in India were Captain W. F. Smith, Captain R. B. Aldridge, Lieut. Wyndham Neave, and Ensign C. B. Murray, 2 sergeants and 24 rank and file killed, 1 officer, Colonel W. Hope, C.B., 4 sergeants, and 50 rank and file wounded. Major H. Loftus, Lieut. and Adjutant Cowburn, Ensign Swainson, and Surgeon W. Simpson, and about 250 men, died of disease. About a half of the loss incurred by disease occurred during the six weeks that the Central India campaign lasted, and during the six weeks that the cholera was raging in the regiment in 1860.

The depôt companies joined the regiment in Edinburgh, and the establishment of the regiment was fixed at 12 companies, with 54 sergeants, 31 buglers and pipers, and 700 rank and file.

1865. In October occurred the death of Brevet Lieut.-Colonel Parker, of typhoid fever, after a service of 23 years in the regiment.

1866. In February, authority was received from the Commander-inChief for the officers of the regiment to wear a sword with a cross hilt instead of a basket hilt on all occasions except at levees, &c.

In the same month the regiment embarked at Granton, for Aldershott, where it arrived on the 19th, and remained stationed there till December, when it proceeded to Portsmouth, and embarked on board Her Majesty's ship " Tamar " for Ireland, where it arrived on the 14th. The head-quarters and five companies proceeded to Fermoy, detaching three companies to Cork and two to Ballincollig. During the whole of this year, when a Fenian outbreak was anticipated, the regiment was much broken up into detachments, having at different times sent detachments to the following places :—Cork, Ballincollig, Mallow, Millstreet, Dungarvan, Mitchelstown, Tralee, Limerick, Killarney, and Rathkeale. On the 27th of November Colonel W. Hope, C.B., retired on half-pay, after a service of 32 years in the regiment, and after having commanded it for eight years, much and deservedly respected and regretted by all ranks. The command now devolved on Major J. J. Macdonell.

1868. The regiment proceeded to Dublin on the 30th April, 1868, at which time its establishment was increased to 800 privates. On the 22nd of July the regiment proceeded to the Curragh Camp, and remained there till the 17th of October, when it embarked on board Her Majesty's ship " Simoom " for Gibraltar, where it arrived on the 22nd of the same month.

1869. On the 1st of April the establishment of the regiment was reduced by 100 privates.

1870. On the 31st of March the regiment sustained the loss by death of Lieut.-General the Honourable C. Grey, the Colonel of the regiment. General Grey had previously commanded the regiment from 1833 to 1842, and had always taken the greatest interest in its welfare. He was succeeded by Lieut.-General R. Law, K.H., who in the earlier part of his military career had served in the Seventy-first during the whole of the war in Spain, having been present with the regiment at all the actions in which it was engaged, and having been wounded several times. He was also severely wounded by a cannon ball at the battle of Waterloo, whilst performing the duties of adjutant. On the 1st of April the establishment of the regiment was reduced from 12 to 10 companies.

According to a return furnished to the Horse Guards in 1872, the Seventy-first proved to be the most national one among the Highland corps, the numbers being 710 Scotch, 25 English, and 18 Irish.

By general order dated 17th March, 1873, the regiment was associated with the Seventy-eighth Highlanders (Ross-shire Buffs), and formed into the Fifty-fifth Brigade, together with the Ross, Caithness, &c., and Inverness, Nairn, and Elgin militia regiments, with its depôt established permanently at Fort George.

On the 24th of April the service companies embarked on board Her Majesty's ship "Tamar," for passage to Malta, where they disembarked on the 30th of the same month.

On the 10th of May the death of Lieut.-General Law took place. He was succeeded in the command of the regiment by Lieut.-General the Honourable G. Cadogan, who was transferred from the 106th at his own request. General Cadogan is nephew of Lieut.-Colonel the Honourable H. Cadogan, who commanded the regiment throughout the whole of the Peninsular war, and was finally killed at the battle of Vittoria

1876. The regiment still remains quartered at Malta. The composition and nationality of the regiment at the present date is as follows:—

Mode of Enlistment.	English.	Irish.	Scotch.	Total.
Enlisted for Seventy-first ...	12	6	526	544
Transfers from other regiments	7	3	—	10
From schools	7	—	—	7
Fifty-fifth Brigade	34	25	—	59
Total ... .. '	60	34	526	620

It will be seen by the above how little the Seventy-first has profited by the Depôt Brigade system.

www.ingramcontent.com/pod-product-compliance
Lightning Source LLC
Chambersburg PA
CBHW030400170426
43202CB00010B/1431